Almira Kidd, Harry Houdini Collection

Psychology, Re-Incarnation, Soul, and its Relations

The laws of being - showing the occult forces in man - that intelligence

manifests without material : and the most important things to know

Almira Kidd, Harry Houdini Collection

Psychology, Re-Incarnation, Soul, and its Relations
The laws of being - showing the occult forces in man - that intelligence manifests without material : and the most important things to know

ISBN/EAN: 9783337780319

Printed in Europe, USA, Canada, Australia, Japan

Cover: Foto ©Thomas Meinert / pixelio.de

More available books at **www.hansebooks.com**

PSYCHOLOGY; RE–INCARNATION; SOUL,
AND ITS RELATIONS;

OR,

THE LAWS OF BEING:

SHOWING

THE OCCULT FORCES IN MAN; THAT INTELLIGENCE
MANIFESTS WITHOUT MATERIAL; AND THE
MOST IMPORTANT THINGS
TO KNOW.

Know Thyself, is the First Essential of Nature's Law.

BY ALMIRA KIDD.

———◆———

BOSTON:
COLBY & RICH, PUBLISHERS,
9 MONTGOMERY PLACE.
1878.

INDEX.

———

4   *INDEX.*

PART II.

INTRODUCTORY.

ONE of the first obligations we owe as moral beings is to render to our fellow-man as much of good as comes within our power to transmit. He who has lived to mature life, and has failed to benefit his fellow-men, has certainly lived in vain, and will some time discover his sin of omission.

These pages are dedicated to the enlightenment of humanity on some of the most important subjects of being.

"Know thyself" is the first law. Learn cause first, and the effects will be readily comprehended as time moves on.

The psychology of man's nature, and the theory of re-incarnation, are rarely taken into account as the first principle of cause. So far as the writer knows, it has never been presented with any clearness, nor approach to a proper defining of its object, aim, or necessity, so essential to a thorough understanding of the subject. In this we hope to make it plain, instructive, and interesting. The subject is one of vast interest to minds that are searching for knowledge in metaphysics and biology, in cause and effect; and to such this will be an assistant and guide. Others can not appreciate the law of progression and the economy of life; and to such we trust these

5

pages will convey many lessons of truth. The subject is one of many ramifications; and the writer never could have taken the task upon herself, of attempting its elucidation, had she not been assisted by higher powers. With her, these lessons commenced years ago; and the information herein presented has been received by means of clairaudience and telegraphy with higher and advanced intelligences, the writer being a general clairaudient and mental telegrapher to mundane and supermundane minds, demonstrated illustrations of the truth of the statements being given at the same time. This was the writer's only source of information.

Living in an uncultured territory, where there were no accessibilities to libraries, nothing could be borrowed to draw from: it is given purely as received. The authorities are not known to myself; my guides saying, "Truth, not authorities, is all-essential." That these lessons come from intelligences far removed beyond the ordinary mode of communicating is certain to the recipient. They are not from spirits in near bondage to earth's conditions, — those who are not emancipated from the prejudices they carried with them, — but from spirits beyond that sphere; although the former are learning, like us, as will be seen by the reader of these pages.

Spirits who are free from the earth's conditions are called "intelligences." Such are in rapport with us and all space by telegraphy, through which they convey ideas, and give impressions. This system of communication is not perceptible to many, because not externalized to the sense. These intelligences, upon approaching us, can not remain in the same atmosphere for any length of time, the rude conditions of carnal life being unsupportable: hence intermediate spirits are employed as channels of communicating, and telegraphy is practical to all who can use it.

As there are spirits in form as intelligent as some out of form, none are excluded; and generations to come will be better informed by means of this direct intercourse.

By this line of communicating, no long discourse is kept up. Short and expressive messages are from the more distant and advanced spheres. The residents of those realms express themselves without prolixity: the ideas are concise, calling for no effort to comprehend, each word conveying its application. As soon as obscurity, inflated language, pretentious long-wording, or attempt to be profound, are displayed, I invariably regard the spirits in communication as false *savants*, and say, " It is not clear ; I can not receive it: " for the language of the spheres is simple, poetic, and emphatic.

There are those who will say re-incarnation is denied by some mediums under control of spirits ; and it is not acknowledged by many others who claim to know something of spiritual things. Granted. But how many spirits on the other side who control mediums are there who know more of the laws of cause than they did before the change? Hardly any. They know their present state, and that is all : and many of them, when they control a medium, take on more strength ; they take on the magnetic forces of the medium, as well as borrow of his or her intellect.

I know one who has been in spirit-life forty-five years, who is yet doting and moping in the old conditions of earth. I have heard an old spirit say that for fully a hundred years after his transit he took no notice of spirit-things, but lived wholly with the people of his tribe on earth, and could not realize higher conditions. Yet such are often taken as good authority. Such spirits will often control a person, and deny the truth and reasonableness of statements that do not conform to their limited knowledge while in the first class. A B C spirits of earth they still are. To all such we say, "Bide thy time."

The question of spirit-existence hereafter is just as manifest to me as that day and night alternate. I see, hear, feel, sense, and hold just as intimate conversation with those of another world as with those on earth, and have them as visitors for days and weeks at a time. The best and the only advice I would give to all those who doubt spirit-intercourse is, "Investigate personally for yourself; for conviction of its truth, thus attained, can alone give you satisfaction."

As the author of these pages, it may not be out of place to say, I am not a public medium; have never been before the public in any capacity or profession, but rather secluded; never was entranced in my life; never unconscious in sickness or health, other than that which accompanies natural, normal sleep; never took a narcotic in my life, nor a stimulant. All the senses have been in full activity while cognizant of the phenomena related in these pages. Whatever is given that may seem singular or surprising is nevertheless true to a syllable, as I know, have experienced, or been informed. I would not be guilty of presenting false ideas on so important a subject to my fellow-beings; for I sense keenly my responsibility and my accountability hereafter. As the work is compiled from knowledge and experiences, it is unavoidable that these experiences are used to demonstrate some of the subjects treated: this must be the apology for using them.   .

Treatises, conjectures, hypotheses, have been profusely used by teachers to indoctrinate theories in humanity. Such are not herein set up. It is absolute facts given, — demonstrated illustrations, simple to the commonest understanding. Such are wanted, not mere theories.

While it is our endeavor to treat the subject in as concise and comprehensive a manner as will convey an understanding of the truth sought to be demonstrated, one part only leads to another, and none can be omitted. Brevity is best suited to general readers; and for such this volume is intended, with the hope that all may find in its pages a solution of some things that have hitherto been to them as mysteries.

> Thus to all is given the light of reason to go by.
> Let reason judge, and weigh each and every cause;
> For *ipse dixit*, so profound, has no reason in their cause.

CLAIRAUDIENCE.

As these pages are given through the lessons conveyed by clairaudience, it will not perhaps be out of place to give a short statement of how this power is exercised.

There are several phases and grades of clairaudience, from the simple whisperings of near spirits in close rapport with the elements surrounding us in the circumambient conditions, to the more distant in space, extending to the more general and universal mind.

Mind expresses itself by thought, and that thought is language. Thought, then, is the expression of the mind's ideas. The external expressions of those ideas are made through and by the tongue and vocal organs in order to reach some other external and material object. That those thoughts and ideas exist without the use of those organs, every one knows. Very many authors and writers can express themselves and convey their ideas better in writing than by oral language. Mind or thought is the intellectual exercise of our spirit-nature, the intelligence within us. It can express itself as well to the internal or spirit side of life as to the external through the vocal organs.

Ideas concentrated and expressed, either by embodied or disembodied minds, will travel through space to their object by vibration, just the same as sound passes to the external ear. It is not necessary to see an object in order to hear the expression of its sound which may come from a distance : the vibration of thought extends beyond the limitations of sound, through the atmosphere.

This is the manner of communicating through the spirit-spheres from one grade to another grade below the range of the former, conveying to it information received from far-distant intelligences ; and in this way the will of the Infinite is made known to all.

Many persons fail to distinguish between intuition, impression, and audition ; affirming there is no true clairaudience except in sound on the atmosphere, or when materialized voice is given by spirit, which may be sound. The writer knows the distinction of these phrases, having been intuitive, impressional, and inspirational from childhood, and developed to clear-hearing, even to the extent of audible spirit-language addressed to the external ear ; and is aware of the extent, power, and scope of this occult force ; for such it truly is.

Those who hear the spirit-language in their immediate presence are not uncommon ; but general auditive persons hear from all directions, the same as disembodied spirits in space : such are rare and exceptional.

It is difficult to convey to the understanding of another the exact idea of its operation, only to represent it as a telegraph, the mind being the instrument at each end of the current. The best illustration, and almost an exact correspondence, of these processes and results, is shown in the recent exhibit of the telephone between Boston and Salem, Mass., where the language, sound of voice, and musical performance, were transmitted between audiences eighteen miles apart through and by the means of the telephone applied to electricity. In no wise dissimilar is the process of the human mind itself, constituted on the same electric principles. All distances are annihilated, and intelligences can be drawn from the distant sun. I have heard distant voices, that seemed to come from immensity itself, of the most awe-inspiring significance, conveying lessons to spirits, which they called the voice of God. In fact, it made me tremble, and feel as though I were hearing the voice of infinitude.

An idea is imaged in the mind : hence, when a distant intelligence fixes its thought on an object or being, it is in rapport with it ; and, if that object is clear enough to be sensitive to it, it will receive the impression.

The universe is like a sounding-board, and will vibrate to the requirements of its souls. To that soul that is aspiring, seeking knowledge, it will impart : to that not capable of receiving, it will withhold. There is no truer maxim, " Seek, and ye shall find ; ask, and it shall be given unto you."

This work is not given exclusively on the basis of hearing, but jointly with that of seeing : the vision would open while hearing the teachings, and at the same time see them illustrated. For instance, the course and advance of the soul from its primitive taking-on of matter, in its progressive stages, was represented moving as up the steps of a ladder, round by round in its ascent.

I do not pretend to say that any thing like the expression or language used is herein given : it is only the substance, theory, and ideas conveyed. I could not retain the expression, as it could not be taken down while listening, and is far superior in beauty and understanding to any transcription of it I could possibly make. Deeming the instruction of interest to others as well as myself, it is given to humanity in these pages.

THEORIES CONTRASTED ON THE LAWS OF BEING.

As the object of this work is to show the origin and progress of the soul in its connection with matter, and the laws of being, I find it necessary to give a graduated synopsis of the tenets and theories most conspicuous among English readers. We will not enter into remote times, but consider only those held by Christian nations of our own. All races and worshipers have held some theory of their origin. The Christian nations and worshipers take the Hebrew Bible as their rule of belief. Of late years, atheists, materialists, and scientists called Darwinians, theorize that man is physically developed from animal forms, starting from the mollusk, developing through various higher forms to vertebrate, thence to mammal, into man. This theory implies a procreation of one type with another, and that one type by amalgamation with another will produce higher germs. This is antagonistic with all of Nature's laws, open to every individual observer. It was never yet seen that different types of creatures would produce by procreating other types; the whole animal world contradicts the theory: while it is shown to every observer that the offspring of different species are infertile. And this extends even to the human kind, as witness the mulatto with a mulatto, who rarely have offspring. The same is observable in the half-breed Indian of the same grade. You may produce a cross between species and genera as mixed bloods; and types improve by selection, as every farmer knows. Nature, no doubt, has carried on this improvement, and is yet doing the same.

Typal germs, however, will never merge into each other. They are eternal entities which Nature takes care of and preserves. The germ of form in man, as well as in the lower animal, is transmitted from one matured world or planet to another. In every sense, the lower animal life is governed by the same natural law as man. In these pages the relationship between man and the lower forms is shown, while progress is recognized as the law governing all.

The next class of theorists worthy of notice are the Liberals, the Spiritualists, and others, all about tending the same way of theorizing : to wit, —

One will say, " Man is an emanation, a spark from the divine Mind, a projectile of his intelligence." Another says, " The soul of man is a divine, etherealized portion of the infinite Over-Soul." What the "infinite Over-Soul " may be is not well explained. Another says, " Man is a luminous emanation of the divine Idea." These all agree that the spirit of man has existed during all time, coeval with this " divine Mind," and that, all these myriad years of time, man was waiting to take earthly form.

Another theory is, " He had a pre-existence as spirit on many planets, then incarnated on this earth like a fallen spirit."

Spiritualists uniformly claim progression in consort with these theories ; and the " divine " in this application is intended to mean the transcendent God. These theorists never except nor exclude any part of humanity from the same common descent. It requires no stretch of vision to look around and see humanity in all its forms as a typal divine emanation. The Patagonians, the blacks of Australia and Africa, the South-sea Islanders, the Diggers, and the Flat-head Indians of the Pacific slope, not mentioning the very low representatives in other races, are, according to this theory, types allied to the divine Archetype, God, — " etherealized portions of the infinite Over-Soul." This theory is blended with progression; yet it is progression downwards, not upwards. It is really retrogression. No simile can be drawn from it, no comparison exist to justify the claim. There is no attribute in man, as seen on earth, that in the remotest degree approaches such a being.

In fact, let them answer how man can be a progressive being, and yet emanate from a "divine Mind," an " etherealized part of God," a perfect being whom you cannot go beyond. Can infinitude be surpassed? It is asserted that man had a pre-existence in other and higher spheres, and became incarnated on this earth as a " fallen spirit." What retrogression is this, to bring spirit down from a higher to a lower condition on earth! If man has had this "pre-existence, or undertone of existence, as part of the divine Mind," is it the first incarnation? If such a course is taken for progression, then earthly matter must be superior to spirit. While these theorists of pre-existence, all-time existence, one coeval with the "divine Idea," show no higher aims or results, their theory is evidently that of retrogression.

In contradistinction to the preceding theories, this work will endeavor to show that soul is an entity in the ocean of all soul, in the depth of darkness, where it gives life to form in the lowest animal states, and moves to higher by stages, round after round, acquiring knowledge of external things, and intelligence of the laws of nature and matter, continually, by and through these changes; and by this method advances to the divine.

Progression, as taught and illustrated in these pages, may be briefly stated as follows : —

Forms are distinctive typal germs in the ocean of matter, represented in worlds before this.

No two beings are exactly alike, because they have not imbibed of the same conditions.

Soul learns the laws and conditions of matter through diversity of forms.

Spirit is the result, the ultimate, of the soul's progress through matter to intelligence.

Soul is the moving power of intelligence in all beings.

Intelligence transcends matter ultimately.

Therefore soul is a distinctive principle from nature and matter, showing instinct, intuition, inspiration, and aspiration; by progressive stages moving on to reach infinitude.

PROLEGOMENA.

A knowledge of one's self is to the human family one of the most important subjects that can concern it, — its origin, advancement, and destiny.

It is with a full sense of the necessity of knowledge, truthfulness, and the benefits to be derived from giving to others as it is given to us, that this work is offered to the public. It sets forth no theory or conjecture of her own, but lessons conveyed to the writer for the period of one year, in short communications from intelligences overreaching the ordinary circumambient spirit-sphere, and at stated times by direct intercourse with and in the immediate presence of spirits, who illustrated the principles given with proof on various occasions, which proof will be shown as we proceed.

These are not second-handed nor intermediate communications, but have been given to the writer in a conscious normal state, and left for her to compile into systematic order; during which compilation the intelligences, when essential, gave more light on the subject and its bearings. In this way is given what the occult world will reveal to mankind.

The theory or doctrine of metempsychosis and transmigration of soul is as old as we have any record in history of the ideas of soul held by mankind. Philosophers of old promulgated it; various classes of worshipers adopted it; and at the present time various classes and tribes believe in the soul's change of habitation.

Where could this theory originate, or how take hold of the imagination of so many, if it had no foundation in truth? Though, like all great truths, it may be emasculated by transmission, and take a deformed shape, yet it shows the persistent effort of soul-intelligence, or spirit, to ingraft the truth of continued life, motion, and progression, on the human mind. Where there is a thing concealed, there must be a key to unlock the door to the secret, so that the door may be placed ajar, and all who will may look within; for a knowledge of all hidden things is to be attained, sooner or later, by all.·

The human mind is not capable of grasping all knowledge at one flash: it, like all things else, progresses by degrees. Therefore it is old and advanced intelligences in spirit that are capable of handling the key to the secret chambers of soul-life and spirit-development. It is not to be expected of all alike, or that all spirit has the same standard of knowledge; for spirit has to learn, as well as flesh.

It is not germane to our subject to review any of the old theories on metempsychosis or transmigration. They are none of them clothed as they should have been to give the idea, and are looked upon by most minds as the vagaries of ignorant tribes and of the dark ages. Metempsychosis and transmigration mean one and the same thing, notwithstanding what may be said to the contrary. The two words were adapted by different classes to convey the same idea; and the meaning is, the transition of the soul from one state of being to another in material form, — it may be in advanced human form, or in that of the brute family.

The ancient theory on metempsychosis was, that immediately at the demise of the occupied body the soul entered
some other form, without allowing any rest or interval of
time to elapse between one occupancy and the other, the
soul being kept in continual motion by this transmigration;
that it depended on the merits or demerits, the character
and quality, of the person, what their subsequent condition
would be. It is not recorded that the ancients could realize the existence of spirit out of form; there was no conception of spirit associated with man: hence the two
spheres were separate; and any visitors by apparition were
considered to be angels or gods, beyond and far above
humanity.

It will be seen, in following our remarks on this subject,
wherein this idea was a misconception and a transposition
of the germs of truth. So we let the dead past bury itself in silence, and take the living present for our theme.
We discard these old terms, and take re-incarnation to be
a migration of the soul from a lower to some higher form;
never allowing that a soul retrogrades from human to
brute life, but that its law is to move in progressive advancement, this being done through various and many
forms.

As this is likely to be the accepted theory of the progressive ages, it may be stated with some exactitude of
limit. Re-incarnation is the habiting of the soul the
second and third time in human form on the same planet.
This is possible to take place the fourth time; but yet this
is so immaterial, it is hardly worthy of our present consideration.

This theory is not new to those who accept the teachings of the Bible; for it may be found inculcated in numerous passages of the old and the new books. As instances,
we quote a few of the many that might be presented, had
we room.

Matt. xvii. 12 : " But I say unto you, That Elias is come
already, and they know him not."

Mark ix. 13 : " But I say unto you, That Elias is indeed
come."

John viii. 58 : " Jesus said unto them, Verily, verily, I
say unto you, Before Abraham was, I am."

John xi. 25 : " Jesus said unto her, I am the resurrection and the life : he that believeth in me, though he were
dead, yet shall he live."

This passage should have read as it was expressed by
him : " I am the resurrected and the living : he that believeth I am, the same shall he be ; " that is, though he
were dead to that form, yet he would fill another form.

Nowhere in the Bible can the resurrection mean the
raising of the same disintegrated first body, as some pro-
fess to believe ; but the raising of soul in some other form,
either in spirit, or again on earth.

It is evident that the fifteenth chapter of the First of
Corinthians teaches that the spiritual resurrection is all
that was expected.   The 45th verse of this chapter might
well serve as a text for our subject: " The first man,
Adam, was made a living soul: the last Adam was made
a quickening spirit."

This passage gives the idea that re-incarnation conveys.
Adam is the common name for a soul incarnated in the
human form.   The first taking of human form, "Adam,"
is a living soul: the last appearance of " Adam " is a
quickening spirit filled with the light of terrestrial knowledge and celestial intelligence, and a spirit that will move
in spheres common to both.   Such is what the writer
evidently knew, and intended to convey.   It is not our
province to search the Scriptures : let those who are
familiar with them search them out.

Of the late writers, many have written newspaper arti-

cles *pro* and *con*, theorizing on the subject; but, as this is
not a review, we pass them by. The most noticeable
writer upon re-incarnation was the French spiritist, Allan
Kardec, who enthusiastically presented it as a dogma.
He gave a theory respecting it in conformity with teachings received through divers media. Yet he affirms it was
" in consonance with his conception and intuition of the
law of a just and merciful God, and he would not have
received it as given if not in harmony with his rational
conclusions."

But we opine that his mediums must have been psy-
chologized by his will or chain of thoughts on that subject;
for we cannot conceive how any spirits, who knew of what
they claimed to treat of, could have conveyed such pue-
rile and inconsistent statements on theosophy and spirit
hierarchy, and so much that is irreconcilable with an-
thropological laws.

Nowhere does he find the integral principle of the soul,
the first essential of the doctrine ; but he confuses it with
spirit, and *vice versa.* He represents spirit as a creation
of God, as one of his secrets neither to be looked into nor
found out. The law of spirit and its conditions does not
begin to be conveyed in its true light. The first requisite
to be explained is made obstruent by referring to them as
God's great secret, not to be known outside of himself,
and that it is a sacrilege for his creatures to inquire into
his works. Allan Kardec had evidently been of Roman-
Catholic faith. His writings are all shaded with its dogmas. A personal God is the rocky foundation he builds
upon ; saints in abundance ; a local, intermediate world
while in transit of expiation. Re-incarnation is made a
state of expiation, and " is the retribution of a just and
merciful God for sin." It is virtually made to be a substi-
tute for a literal hell to produce purification. Moral purity

is the graduating scale that decrees what you will next be. Intelligence has little weight, and the highest intellect may next be a bonded slave or a Fuegan. In fact, it is made a system of literal punishments clear through, to be carried out on earth; and this is the only object that is clearly conveyed in all of his writings upon the subject.

His theory is without order or system, making life erratic, as he represents the unpurified spirits to be. The psychometrical law is not touched as a cause, nor is progress hinted at.

As this work was in manuscript before seeing his, and they bear no comparison in treating the subject, but are radically different, no further allusion will be made to it but where the difference exists can be readily seen. That re-incarnation is a psychological law, as sublime in its economy as it is worthy of man's consideration, will be understood as we progress in knowledge and understanding.

PART I.

WHAT IS GOD?

THE races and classes of beings of all ages of time have adopted some specific form or idea of a God. These ideas have been as diversified, almost, as humanity itself; and as many gods have been set up to worship as the requirements of the worshipers demanded. Many of the present day picture a great transcendent personality; others, a Deity in a central sun, moving all the universe from it as a centre; and so on *ad infinitum*. But now that the two spheres of earth and spirit are in close rapport, and converse is familiar, humanity is no better informed on this subject of a personal God than before. No spirit has as yet reported to have found a personal Deity. The highest intelligences can not inform us of such a being. That there is a power or principle governing the actions and conditions of things is true: no one in earthly form knows this better than the writer, who has seen its action in spirit-life. Yet we by no means attribute this to one being or deity. It must be taken into consideration, that, if time has been always, there must be some spirits who have been for an inconceivable period moving on towards infinitude. That such exercise a

21

combined influence of intelligence on mundane and supermundane life is true. It is a concentrated power as
well; but this concentration of power is not what is
represented to be the great First Cause, — God of the
universe, Maker and Ruler of all things.

Intelligences have never discovered the personal of a
God more than these before mentioned. God is supposed
to fill all the universe as an infinitude: therefore Nature
and her works are supposed to be the best similitude of
an infinitude. Nature's laws and works can not be in-
fringed upon nor varied: all things are subject to them:
therefore it best conveys to us the idea of God.

There is a concentration of intelligence of a far-reaching
power; but it is only intelligence that has passed through
Nature's laws in matter and form for a series of ages not
to be computed. This centre of light has the attributes
of a far-reaching power of vision, by which it is enabled
to see all conditions relating to spirit and its records, to
make itself felt and heard, and is in communication with
all intermediate spheres, with ability to convey to each
one or all what is for them to know, either in earth or in
spirit. These communications are conveyed like a voice
in the far distance, and many spirits call it the voice of
God. In this way the lower spheres know there is something far beyond them of force, knowledge, and power;
and many call it God; but it is properly the spirit-centre.

Question. — How or where is this centre?

Answer. — The sun is the centre of our system, and the
object towards which spirit and planets are travelling. It
casts its influence on spirit-space as well as on the conditions of earth. It is a centre of light and intelligence;
and that is all it is essential now to remark of it. Nothing herein is intended to convey an idea that it is a deity.
There are other suns and systems. An infinite God must
be a unit.

SOUL AND ITS IMPORTANCE.

No theme is more profound, nor of deeper moment to humanity, than that of the law of being.

Theorist, *savant*, and scientist of various schools have given their views of it; but none of them stand the test of reason when investigated by some other rule : the foundation is found to be of sand, and their structure hardly outlives the constructors. The weakness of these is to ignore the true basis, the hidden principle : they are mostly materialists, and show but one side of natural law, and that the weakest. The cause and action of the intelligent part remains unaccounted for. Why it shows itself in such a diversity of ways, and why it is just as active outside of form after its demise, is more than their laws of matter will explain ; and, until this hidden cause is made plain, there is no solid foundation for theories of " essences," " Over-Soul," "emanations," or " divine ideas." Materialists or Darwinians, these unsatisfactory structures must soon fall from their own weakness.

Of the humbler and less pretentious, the ignorant and illiterate tribes, to the very lowest grades of humanity, generally believe there is some force, essence, or principle in them that has a past, present, and future condition ; and in some theories they come nearer the truth than do the higher classes. It would appear, that, the nearer humanity is to Nature, the better her laws are understood ; but, when it soars to realms of speculation, it loses itself in mistiness.

Although soul is commonly spoken of, and spirit equally as much so, yet it is rarely that a distinction is made between the two ; many thinking them to be synonymous terms, that cannot be separated in meaning or purpose : where one is, both are.

It is our design to show that there is a distinction and a difference : one may be without the other.

Although soul clothes itself with spirit, yet the spirit of things may be without soul. All soul moves to and with intelligence : all spirit may not. Soul is diversified and progressive : all spirit is not. Many things of spirit are without soul, to speak in the literal, just, and true sense.

A great confusion is made of this theme by psychometrists, who will tell you of the soul of an inanimate, impersonal, unintelligent thing. They will handle some rock, wood, or metallic substance, and read what they term its soul ; and the impress made on any thing is designated by the same term : not distinguishing that the soul is within themselves, that reads the conditions, elements, and surroundings of the thing they handle or come near to, which cannot be detected by one in a thousand, and therefore is not thrown off by the thing itself ; for, if it were, it could be commonly perceived by others as well.

As we learn of the true nature of the soul, its attributes and purposes, it should not be confounded with all unintelligent things ; for its distinguishing characteristics are instinct and intelligence.

Spiritualists make little account of the soul-principle. In this they do less than theologians, who recognize soul to be of the first importance ; and in reality it is primary to intelligence, and makes the identity of our being throughout time. It is the soul-principle that gives us spirit, spiritual life and progress, etc. Spiritualists reverse this important fact, and give spirit all power of being and importance ; whereas spirit is only the condition the soul has made, the form it is seen through, and an indicator of its rate of progress. It is the soul that retains its identity through eternity, not spirit only so far as it is a part of the soul's knowledge of itself.

The spirit from the animal life is dispersed, as soul drops it for progress in other forms of advancements ; and this is done again and again.

The soul clothes itself with matter in form for progress, character, and practical knowledge of the laws of matter and external life. These combined make its expression of spirit, and its claim for further attainment of knowledge.

Question. — Some writers assert that the life principle is force or motion, the same as electricity. Are their assertions true?

Answer. — The action of the soul is electro-dynamic ; but this is not the primary cause of its expression. Electricity is force or motion ; but these are not promotive of intelligence in any form where instinct and judgment are required for its sustenance and preservation. There is a special principle that gives the expression, which is a divine principle, and is imbued with all power to sustain itself and acquire intelligence without dependence, or being subject to laws of force. It has been in existence for all time, but individualized only from the time of its first habiting itself with matter, having previously existed only as an entity of one whole.

To illustrate, take an orange. Its substance is divided into strands, seeds, and innumerable small tuberculous membranes filled with its substance, compactly put together in a sphere, inclosed in one rind. Yet each of these small tubercles is an entity, and can be picked out by itself. It, however, contains the identical substance of that one orange, when all together, forming one whole, with the same flavor and principle throughout. Such is the comparative relationship that each individual soul-life bears to each other, as a unit of one common principle. Experience, development, and its career, make its individuality.

Question. — What is the distinguishing principle, what the attributes, of the soul?

Answer. — The distinguishing principle is that innate nature in man that conveys a power to gain intelligence. Its attributes are of that character that give power to discern, to choose, to learn, and the essential requisite to develop to a higher state of intelligence. The object of its mission is, by experience to acquire education through various conditions and the processes of Nature's laws. It is not a distinctive, conscious individuality, only as it takes form; the first expression it makes always being in the lowest, thence moving to higher developments. This, be it understood, belongs to the animal life, and is not associated with the mineral, vegetable, or oceanic life. These last are confined to matter and its development within the radius of the sun's rays, which always carry magnetic force to any thing they reach not intelligent. In the animal world where life is established, its individuals depend more on their own resources, and derive their sustenance from natural laws.

Soul, then, may be considered to be in motion, let it be in ever so small a thing. Be it no larger than a canary, it is expressive of a soul-principle that may be educated to more or less intelligence, and must retain an existence after the demise of its earthly form.

Question. — What are the soul movements, and object?

Answer. — Soul is without form or gender until it is clothed with matter. Its first movements are in the first elements of matter in the animal being, aggregating to itself the elements and intelligence of these forms, and so on through a multiplicity of forms, in order to reach the desired standard. It is not essential for one to take all forms in the lowest being, but only the essential that will give intelligence sufficient to attaining to that in which it will next become manifest. This accounts for the various character of expression from the human soul, some taking more of one element in nature, and so expressing itself according to the elements it most assimilates with. In this way, soul is educated to its grade of manifesting. Its object is to overcome obstacles, and control matter in all formations; to learn the laws that operate through Nature, and gain intelligence.

Question. — What is the first condition of consciousness?

Answer. — There is no individual consciousness until externalized: it is a principle in one whole, not conscious of self: its state is darkness, nudity, and inaction. Unconsciousness in the ethers of matter is acted on by spirit, and develops consciousness.

Question. — Spirit, then, is the energizing principle?

Answer. — Spirit is the energizing principle of the universe, not of intelligence.

Question. — What, then, is?

Answer. — Soul is the intelligent principle that actuates spirit.

Question. — Is there any centre, sun, or being, from which this principle emanates?

Answer. — None. It pervades the universe.

MEMORY AND INTELLIGENCE.

Memory is a faculty of mind to retain knowledge or ideas. It is an attribute of the soul, and is inherent in it as part of its divine essence. It constitutes its intelligence, and only as such is it practically utilized from one state to another. It is not essential that all the conditions should remain: these conditions are lost in the æons of time that it is in transition. We change our condition even in the short life we have in the present state on earth: what changes, then, are possible to us in inconceivable periods of time!

It can not be shown that any thing in the animal life is wanting in memory. Animals will show what has once displeased, or seeks what has gratified them. If they did not exercise memory, their haunts and progeny would be forgotten, and life would be the daily gratifying of wants, without order or distinction: all would be forgotten from hour to hour. On the contrary, we know that some animals have remembered persons and things for years. There is hardly an animal that cannot be trained, to more or less extent, to know the conditions you wish them to become subject to; and they may be educated to a remarkable degree of intelligence. How could this be done without memory?

This demonstrates that memory is common to all animal life. Why, then, should it become extinct in them, and not in man? They are subject to the same laws of life, the same elements sustain them, as man; yet man can not afford them any place outside of the benefits and services they render to him.

Divine economy has done better than this: Nature and her laws work through them as through us. Man could not have lived on this earth if the animal life had not preceded him.

Intelligence should hardly require defining; but, as it is the indicator of the soul's progress, too much importance can not be given to it. Every change and experience gives knowledge, which is education; and education gives us a power to judge, will, and execute, to be self-governing, and a capacity for higher attainments. It shows what we are, and what we can attain to. It is the grand object of our being, and by slow but ceaseless advancement goes with us through eternity. Memory is the prerequisite of intelligence, and it is self-evident that intelligence is acquired through memory. And yet memory is the distinctive property of the soul. Intelligence is growth and cultivation into knowledge, the ensign of distinction and character. It is just as easy to know what degree of progress a soul has made by its intelligence as it is to tell one stock from another.

There is no more uniformity of acquired knowledge or advancement in spirit-life than we see around us in all directions in physical life, until spirit has acquired it by its further extended life in spheres beyond. Each migration the soul makes carries with it just so much intelligence as it has acquired through that form from which it migrates. This remains by it, and constitutes its spirit-character.

INTELLIGENCE *VS.* MATTER.

Intelligence being that distinguishing property of soul from unintelligent matter or spirit, it necessarily follows that it is not common to all matter or all spirit. Materialists, scientists, and others may use all their talent to show that it is only cause and effect, the laws of force on matter, the instinct of animal life, etc. To make their theories hold good, they must disclaim all intelligence outside of matter. As Spiritualism demonstrates to a certainty the many ways of intelligence manifesting without form, it is found necessary by those who would ignore these facts to deny it *in toto*.

That the intelligence that has developed through the force and momentum of matter (by this is meant the external life it has experienced) will act independent of matter will be shown from absolute knowledge in the course of this work, on the veracity and honor of the writer. It will be shown that all intelligence is preserved, and acts for the general benefit of those who can receive it ; that all space is filled with intelligence in action, and is imbibed by all things for which it is suited; that it is taken on and thrown off by those in flesh, is the light of soul to soul, the sympathetic action of kind accessible to all.

To show intelligence *versus* matter, the following experiences are given. In the year 1875, being then in close rapport with spirit-life, many remarkable occurrences took place. One night, retiring about ten, in harmony with my surroundings, I turned to listen to the invisibles present. Shortly, hearing something in the distance, I stretched out on the back; crossed the hands on the breast to listen. A current like a fine draught of air came to the head; at the same time, distant conversation came to me.

Shortly the current came to a small focus at the top of the forehead, and spread, as it extended far into space, in something of the form of a trumpet. Through this channel a steady stream of discourse came to my brain from a far-distant sphere of intelligence, conveying exalted and sublime lessons on the relation of things and the spirit-spheres, — things that I never heard nor conceived of before nor since. This continued in a steady flow for five hours, without vibration or intermission, from eleven to four in the morning, when at the dawn of day it abruptly ceased. I had lain in the same position, without a motion, not so much as that of a finger, save only to look around the room, and was surprised when I saw the dawn of day. The spirits present had listened the same as I. After a few remarks by them on the power I possessed, I turned, and had my morning sleep.

Here was intelligence of the most transcendent character, without form or connection with matter: so far as I could tell, it was as distant as the sun.

I have many times since heard these far-distant intelligences give short lessons, or remarks intended for some spirit present and to myself. But one more example will answer for all.

One day in summer, the house all open to the breeze, engaged at what my affairs required of me, I had present a spirit who was very familiar, — one that had cared for me in my infancy. I said, " Eliza, why don't you let me see you in tangible form? " I meant clear and material.

She instantly said, " I'll do so if you wish."

" Certainly," I replied. I had no sooner said it than I felt the spirit touch me, and the strangest sensation of forces going from me, as though I were opening out. I began to sense a loss of power ; when a loud, powerful voice from afar said, " Eliza, don't draw or take from the medium : you would materialize in that open room, and injure her. It is her intelligence we want to utilize, and not weaken her."

She replied, " I wouldn't injure her if I knew it."

As I took up a piece of work (the trimming of a hat), the intelligence entered into an explanation of what spirit-materialization is, and the manner in which it is done, using the work I had in hand as a means of illustration ; saying, " That material has been used in one form : now it will be used in another by a mere alteration of its shape and appearance. Thus is materialization only taking or changing material from one form into some other form. And so it ever is : matter is transformed and retransformed continually."

The lesson was a beautiful one to both, so plain, and easily understood without questioning. My spirit-friend Eliza appreciated it as I did, while neither of us knew from whence it came. Here was clear practical intelligence projected, as it would seem, from a vacuum.

That intelligence is drawn from and utilized between

those in flesh is equally true. For some years I could not attend a lecture without feeling the most exhausting, sinking lassitude, even to faintness, truly sickening, not being able to account for it. Latterly I went to hear a strong, positive radical. Soon I began to feel a fullness of the brain, while a current, like a thread, went out to him from me. I could feel it like the thread unwinding from the bobbin, and he was drawing it off. Soon I had a violent headache.

I knew a delicate, frail, sensitive woman, who could but rarely go to lectures without losing her strength for several days.

By what law does this operate? may be asked. Simply, the speaker draws from the intelligent forces of his audience, not the words, expressions, or sentiments, but the intelligent principle that helps him to keep up a flow of expression and ideas. It is the magnetic attraction of all entertaining, forcible speakers.

This free expression of intelligence is the exclusive attribute of soul, and not of matter.

It can be shown that gross matter can resolve itself into infinitesimal ethereal particles, going we know not where: this is the spirit of the thing. A shrub, tree, or flower passes off its elements as well as animal life. One must therefore exist in spirit-matter as well as the other. Every gross substance has the same divisibility, but does not express intelligence in one sphere more than the other.

Intelligence is the distinguishing nature of soul.

PROGRESSIVE INTELLIGENCE.

When intelligence is in action, it is thrown off like a principle; and individuals who have the capacity to receive may imbibe of its flow. It is like the putting-on of a garment: you can not wear what does not fit you.

A child does not want strong food until it has capacity to digest it. So it is with soul : all progress is made through external life and experience : development, strength of character, can only be reached by a process of stages, and will not go beyond its strength.

Intelligence advances by degrees and grades, as we see in all our surroundings. The child learns only according to its circumstances. And so with adults : none jump at full knowledge or advancement, but attain it by slow stages : some make little advance, others rapid progress. Even in the same family, where the same opportunities exist, a great difference may be seen. In this particular the soul shows its individual standard, what its capacity or want of strength really is. It may be so constituted, from its line of succession, that it can not over-reach nor pass the bounds in its present form ; while another may reach out and grasp all knowledge in art or science, because it has made progress, through its line of succession, to take in or imbibe the higher gifts, to comprehend ideas of advancement, or to lead in progressive movements. Such manifestations indicate the soul's development, but do not show the limit nor the acme of its capabilities ; for it is the law of life to move on to the attainment of an infinitude of intelligence. All may expect and anticipate in time and eternity to reach the acme of their desires.

The majority of minds reverse this line of progression, and adopt the egotistical presumption that man descends from the God of all infinitude, Spirit of all intelligence and wisdom ; but they fail to show by what line of theory mankind is so diversified in physical, intellectual, and moral standing. Some certainly show very degraded animal parts of the infinite divine Source. If it is his semblance, he would be a great contradiction in character, and partial in gifts and benefits to his descendants. But the truth is, there is no analogy in comparison with such a pretentious claim: mankind nowhere approaches any such standard of being. 'It is only as shown by a series of developments that he acquires traits that can compare in the least degree with those of a divine mind.

History need not be searched to prove the self-evident fact, that the human family is outgrowing superstition, bigotry, and idolatry; throwing off the bonds of serfdom, and submission to faith; becoming independent self-thinkers; reaching out for more knowledge and higher conditions; and fast learning the relation it bears to spirit. These are the signs of man's progressive spirit. They show that he is advancing, not receding; that he has not fallen from some high position, but is reaching upward, and aspiring to higher standing. Let them learn to discard all theology, priestly creeds, and church; assert their own individual priesthood; approach the supreme fount, and satisfy their own souls.

THE ANIMAL WORLD. — ITS USES.

Many in the interest of science and biology have speculated more or less on the part the animal world fills in its being. While some give animals a correlation to man, others deny them any thing but gross matter: when defunct, that is the last of them. No one seems to have found the true purpose of their being, further than in the use they are to man.

Those who have the most to do with animals, and those who are the most observing of them, cannot fail to see that they are capable of a great deal of intelligence when trained and schooled to it. . I make no exceptions here of kind. It is not essential to give examples; for general observation will prove that they exhibit thought, memory, and expression.

By objectors it is said they do not think consecutively, do not plan, do not use language to express ideas, and in many other ways do not resemble man's intellectual ability : all which is only half-way true.

We do not propose to enter into any review of these objections, but show the law that operates through animals in comparison with those operating through man.

We would not claim that the animal's physical structure has latent germs of development to humanity. Every type and species holds its own. Though, physically, animals do not develop to man, the elements that enter into the composition of the animal are taken in by man ; and the intelligence the animal gains is utilized to the same end.

True, the animal is not organized so as to possess the same mental intellect. There is not the development of brain which is the distinguishing, intellectual, spiritual organ in man : therefore they are lower in the scale of development.

Some writers affirm that the animal differs essentially from man, inasmuch as it ever moves in a circle, returning into itself, and not progressing out of its sphere. But this is no more true of animals than of men. Nowhere can it be seen that man goes beyond the circle of his sphere while in his physical form ; and his understanding is trivial compared with what it may be. His intellect can reach only a certain limit, while some even are only removed from the animal in physical shape.

The fact that animals do not change their habits, or a bird its notes or the manner of building its nest, does not indicate a want of intelligence, or inability to progress. There is not a form in external life that can alter its natural adaptability. Man can not change nor move beyond his nature. There is no power of will he can exercise that can enable him to fly, to make himself taller or shorter, or to cover himself with hair; while, if he violates a law of his nature, death ensues. Thus every thing in physical life is subject to the laws and restrictions of its own expression.

Man in his present sphere is an arrested or retarded development, because in another sphere he will surpass the present state. If this is true of man, can it be said of the animals, they will not go beyond their present state?

But let us consider the animals' future state and uses. Their earthly form is subject to the same law as man's. When they die, their matter goes to earth, and their elements into gases.

What are these elements?

They are the ethereal, spiritual substances of matter, and will form material for other organisms; man himself in his own element not being excepted in the action of this law.

Yet some will assert there is no animal in spirit; that only the earthly matter is utilized; that, if there are animals or birds of plumage in the higher spheres, they are indigenous to those spheres, and not products of earth's grossness.

This raises the queries, What is indigenous to spirit-spheres? What is spirit-matter?

There is nothing but reason and example to meet these inquiries.

By the science of chemistry, it is known that every substance can be resolved into its elements, and matter show its primates. The diamond, the hardest known substance, could be dissolved if the process were known. Nature is but one vast laboratory in this work, resolving, dissolving, and reconstructing. Matter that has served one form will enter another. It is only a question of bulk and quality. Matter, therefore, cannot be said to be indigenous to spirit more than to the external, when it is only exchanged; and every thing of earth can be shown to possess an ethereal spirit part.

It is common for spirits to show themselves in garments of every description, and change them to their liking. Are these indigenous to spirit-life?

A spirit entered my door once, wearing a long summer-coat, with the pockets filled with apples, and asked others present if they liked them, while he showed them round. This was characteristic of the man, which I knew as well as himself. He had not laid away his tastes. But of the apples: where did they come from? Did they grow in spirit-spheres? were they indigenous spirit-fruit? They were not; for the spirit told where he culled them: he had appropriated them from bearing trees in Oregon. What had he taken? Why, the essence, the spirit-elements, of the fruit.

On another occasion, the same summer, a spirit entered the door. After talking with others present, he took out his watch to compare the time with my clock on the wall, saying, "I set my watch by the time I am to keep." Are watches manufactured in the spirit-spheres? Not this one, at least. One present whom he was talking to had been his wife in life on earth, and said, "There's his old watch: what an idea to have that watch!"

Another time, this same spirit entering, I immediately saw him, and that he was dressed in what I took to be fine blue cloth, — a dress-suit. I said to others present, "That's a fine cloth suit." — "Not so very fine," they replied: "it's middling.' When he said, "I took them in Hamburg. They just suited me. They are not the finest kind: I picked them out from others in the store for my purpose." Thus these clothes had been appropriated, ready-made and finished to wear, from the stock of some store in Europe. What became of the external, the gross material, these several things were taken from, I never thought to ask.

If inanimate, unintelligent material can be taken up, and utilized in spirit, must the animal be an exception to other matter, and have no purpose but the physical? Let those answer who think such a view consistent.

The animal is not indigenous to spirit-spheres, because there is nothing that is: if there were, it would make a preference and maintain a precedence over humanity. That the animal has its uses, more than its earthly matter would indicate, is equally true as of man. The intelligence the animal gains manifests again in some other form under the same progressive laws. The principle is there. I do not say nor mean the details of memory, the nature, but that the essence, the expression of the principle, moves higher. They are animated by the soul-principle, consistent with the form of external matter they represent.

Much importance and stress is laid on the fact, by objectors, that animals do not exercise language, nor apply it. In this they overlook the fact that all animals will learn to understand the meaning of language from those they are associated with: from the guttural Indian to the elegant Latin, there is not one that animals will not respond to understandingly. If animals will learn the meaning of articulated sounds, words, or expressions, it evidently is proof that something is there that knows or has learned the application of language. They do not use it, because their organic structure will not permit them to do so; and yet they show expression from their own guttural natures. That they show thought, is undeniable: there are too many unquestionable evidences open to every observer to require any further showing of proofs.

It may be asked, Is principle diversified in its action?
Yes. See in what numerous ways hydrogen shows
itself, from the bulky ocean to the imperceptible breathing.

Force is power exerted. In how many inconceivable
ways does it act, from the atom to the moving of worlds!
The principle is the same : the matter acted on constitutes
the diversity.

Electricity is the same, from the action in the atmosphere to the transmitting of thought.

CREATIVE FORCES.

Force has two distinct phases, — the force of atoms,
ethers, or gases; and the intelligent force acting on
matter.

It is commonly affirmed that all matter is moved by the
power of spirit. Not so. All spirit understands some
laws of matter ; but matter may act independent of intelligence. We see the many phases of action of gases : it
is a momentum within itself. Man may plant a shrub, or
sow seed, and work over it as he likes : yet he can produce no results unless other conditions are favorable outside of him, such as earth, light, heat, or climate : these
are forces independent of his control. Spirits are subject to
the same restrictions : they can not supersede the law, but
make use of matter as they perceive it. They act on
matter as we do through life.

Question. — How, in the beginning, did organic animal
or human life exist on this earth? It does not seem rational
that one kind of animal could be the progenitors of another type, or that man could develop from the animal
form. Was the human ever animal, or covered with hair?

Answer. — The human has never been materially different on this planet. Creation in the human and the animal
takes place the same, — in the beginning, by germs of their

kind existing in the ethereal matter of the earth. Soul moves on spirit-essences, and gives vitality; and, by the same power, that vitality is sustained.

It must be remembered, that the formation of worlds is the result of a combination of elements, germs, and matter from antecedent worlds thrown off in space. These constituents, by means of the power of attraction, form other worlds; while the soul-principle acts the same throughout the universe. Spirits are specially interested in these new formations and in the life of the young. Where worlds are forming, spirits are earnestly at work.

Therefore the human species took its place upon the earth distinctively as races, essentially as they are, through germs moved by soul and spirit essences, and sustained until propagated; when, no longer needing the special intervention of spirit in that direction, they were not so forcibly acted upon. Let the earth be wholly depopulated by some catastrophe, and the same process of creation would be renewed.

In this way a great power of forces united with soul presence is acting on germs and matter throughout space the same to-day as in the past. This is creative force.

Question. — Under what law do animal germs exist in space?

Answer. — The germ being the seed of an animal, it is shed by the female. It may be incipient conception, or it may not take root in her substance after impregnation. In the latter case it is wholly useless, but passes to external matter, and so takes its place in the germinal. The innumerable young that are lost fill this place. Each and every substance is conditioned in universal matter; and, for that reason, animal germs are held by the same.

In the first ages of the earth, many forms of life belonged to conditions that do not now inhabit it; and thus it will be in the future. Some that are now common will be extinct, and their tracks will not be detected: the grosser will sink below the superior, and intelligence will predominate. It is the law of progress. Perhaps no science or theory is more mixed by those that expound thereon than the law of evolution and the law of progress. One should not apply to the other; yet it is too frequently done. Evolution is unfoldment, and one of Nature's own laws: it evolves from the elements vegetable, and from vegetable insect and reptile, life. Frogs and mosquitoes only evolve from stagnant water. From marine elements are evolved forms of marine life. These are especially indigenous to the elements that evolve them, and will not exist outside of them. You can not make fishes live out of water; nor tropical fruits, flowers, or the peculiar insects of the tropics, evolve in cold climates. While Nature's infinite law of evolution is illimitable, it is yet restricted to conditions and elements. But this has not the same application to that progress which is advancing by change, and applies to intelligent things. Nature evolves from elements the lower forms. Soul progresses through conditions, is homogeneous to all locations: one is not the other. Evolution is Nature's law on elements. Progress is soul's law of advancing intelligently: this belongs to soul and spirit. Evolution belongs to nature and matter.

SPIRIT LAW AND MATTER.

Let not this heading be considered as implying that any approach will be made to show all of spirit law; for that could not be done in this short lesson, nor contained within the lids of this book. Only a fraction of an idea bearing on this subject can be given.

Spirit here applies to the intelligent principle belonging

to the soul; not the ethereal sublimate of matter called
the spirit-essences of things which perhaps require defining. Spirit-ethers float in space picturing their nature and
kind. These again are imbibed by external things growing in nature, and may be called the essence, or spirit-
part, of things. This ethereal essence again passes out
of these forms as they mature. The same, we perceive
the bloom and the fragrance of the plant, maturing, fad-
ing, and dying out: its spirit-ethers have passed into
space. These again will be imbibed by others as they
develop new forms, whose external growth will make the
demand. In this way there is a continual change and
exchange, a passing-in and throwing-off, a moving of
spirit-essences in and out.

Many claim that spirit is a power giving form to matter;
that it is the real world of things. In opposition it can
be said, spirit develops matter, and material etherealizes
to spirit, — a mutual correlation. This law is applicable
to unintelligent forms.

It is the promulgated theory of Bible-sects, and nearly
all theorists, — spiritualists not excepted, — that man is
descended from some great transcendent power of Deity,
or perhaps fallen angelic beings; and by some, that superior power of spirit is in him before taking earthly form.
By this they mean he had at first the position of spirit to
some extent; that his present state is probational. This
idea has obtained credence from the fact that soul incarnate has a memory of a prior state within itself. Then
it has been used by leaders or teachers in an obscure, half-
intelligent light, and so become perverted. But the reverse
of this is true. As before shown, the soul's first movement is through earthly matter, in order that it may learn
of its uses, and become acquainted with the external
world. This is primary to intelligent growth.

The soul is its own maker, its own creator into spiritual conditions. Every contact, every habiting with form, gives more or less intelligence.

Inasmuch as soul has a common essence to the all-universal Soul, it is made in the image of God and of universal Deity, partaking of a common brotherhood through intelligence; and the same law of origin is applicable to the entire chain of animal life. As it is through matter and form the soul clothes itself with individuality, it necessarily follows that this will be used and persevered in until the proper acme of development and intelligence is reached.

To assert, as some do, that spirit develops and grows in spirit-life the same as with external life, is far from true. Ideas of that kind are conveyed through deceptive spirits who are not able to know beyond the limits of their sphere. A certain development must be through the externals. Spirit must learn the use of material by experience, and can not grow into form in any other way. If angels and seraphim exist, it is only those who have passed through forms the same as we those we occupy, and have been countless ages in attaining their present light. To suppose that man should come down from these advanced lights, as some state, is an egotistical assumption, without a basis for truth.

Believe, then, that you are passing up to, and not that you have descended from, angels; that you are on the high road to become archangels; and that all animal life will follow in your path.

Nothing herein conveyed is intended to imply that spirit fills its measure of attainment in knowledge while associated with external nature; for this is only a preliminary acquirement for continuing the same. Our career may be compared to that of children at school passing from primary to other classes, and so on until they graduate, or pass out : then they are only started to make use of that schooling to aid them through subsequent life to the best advantage.

It is evident from what has been given that intelligent spirit is soul-development, and not a full-fledged bird ready to fly when sent forth from the throne of God. It is, however, the recipient of light, by the aid of which it winds its way, and becomes its own maker.

For this external life is essential ; and the experiences of the soul, in its journey through human life, are absolutely necessary for its unfoldment in its efforts to attain its object. Therefore all entering spirit-life unsatisfied, dwarfed, abortioned, cut off without blooming, will retake external life in form, and make the journey sure.

Each experience gives character, personality, individuality, according to its representation. These convey only the present status, and are not necessarily permanent. We change from decade to decade in this life. We no longer think, look, nor act as children of fifteen or twenty years past. From many the whole *personnel* has gone, and may change three or four times in a hundred years : many change equally as much in character, and would not follow the same path of life a second time. Therefore the details of personality are transitional passages to soul ; and only the experiences they have given make and constitute their identity, which is made manifest by their mode of expression and the light they give.

It must be evident to the reader of these pages that we make a close distinction between soul, spirit, thing, and matter. To say such and such is spirit does not necessarily imply that it is moved by an intelligent soul. Flowers, fruits, scenery, and all tangible things, are taken up in spirit-form. It is a question in the writer's mind, whether the mirage is not a spirit-picture. Spirits say it is ; that the elements are taken up in a rarefied atmosphere, and seen with more facility. If so, it is a fair illustration of external matter giving spirit-essences ; one that is easy of comprehension by all minds. It is plainly evident to all observers, that the rougher, grosser material develops the finer. The grape does not yield the spirit of the wine only through the coarse wood and fibre of the vine. As the ethers and gases can only be brought out through distillation from crude substances, and if imperfect are re-submitted to process, so is it essential with spirit to pass through external matter to reach a higher state. If it has not made its standard suitable for higher spheres, it is re-submitted to another process.

Question. — If external nature is required for development, can there be exceptions, and some attain the same end by shorter journeys, and some even without any, but pass into spirit from the mother's womb, and meet the same results, — a doctrine that is promulgated by many?

Answer. — By no means could this be. Nature, or Nature's God, allows no such infringement on her laws. Such would be spirits without form, too ethereal to find a place. Matter is as utilitarian to spirit-intelligence as to us in earthly form. To spirit it is transparent, and is acted on by them with the facility that a chemist would manipulate a substance he would analyze. This will be best understood by examples.

Several years since, the writer could hardly go to assemblies, large or small, without experiencing the oddest sensations imaginable, — first a weight on the head ; then a slow expansiveness of the whole body, so that it seemed to puff out like a monster, and fill half the room ; then a drawing-in and shrinkage. I knew it was some outside condition, as it never occurred at home. That was as far as I could account for it.

In 1875, when spirits were at home with me, they seemed to vie with each other in efforts to show me all the attention they could bring to bear. One night they said they would show me what it was to disintegrate the body, and dissolve it; asking me if I was not afraid.

I replied, that I was not; that I felt perfectly safe. In a few moments a current ran through me. I began to puff out, and fill the room. Then it seemed that every particle fell asunder, and then came together. The whole process was but for a few minutes. There was no bad result from it or the sensation. But I was thereby enabled to better understand the former sensations. Spirits drew from me certain elements by which they could show themselves to some seer in the assembly, or for some other purpose. More than two years subsequently, one of those exhibiters calling themselves by some long eight-syllable name — which, cut short, means " juggler " — came to the city to exhibit. As I heard he was excellent in his profession, I went to the show. I found him a skillful performer : some of his tricks were spirit-manifestations ; a fact he did not attempt to conceal, calling on his unseen assistants for responses, and through inanimate things to act and show intelligence. At the conclusion he announced that on the next evening he would close his exhibition with his great "Arabic Turkish Box Feat," telling what he intended to perform. As he was half-way honest, not denying he had invisible performers assisting him, I thought I would see his miraculous trick.

His exhibition was in a theater that seated several hundred, and it was filled. I procured a seat immediately in front of the centre of the stage, so that there was nothing intervening between myself and the performance. When it came to the *finale,* a committee of two was to be

selected from the audience to act as judges and inspect-
ors, and show their skill in tying the box and man.
The audience chose two of the strongest men present, one
the sheriff of the county. On the stage was brought a
large, heavy, iron-fastened box, closing with a hasp for a
padlock. This box was to be lashed with as many feet of
rope as they chose to use. It was raised on chairs from
the floor, and fifteen minutes taken to lash it. Then the
sheriff chose to use handcuffs, instead of a padlock, to
fasten the hasp; and, having locked these, he put the key
in his pocket. Then the performer came before the audience dressed in tights, and was to be bound with ropes
as long as they wished, and in any way they pleased.
Several cords were used. He was tied and bound, tight
and immovable. Hands, feet, and legs were corded
together. Then a black cloth bag was put over him, the
string tied at the head, sealed with wax, and stamped.

After this long prelude he was left. The curtains were
drawn around him and the box, shutting the light from
them. The committee sat on the outside. In about
fifteen minutes the bag was thrown over the curtain to one
of the committee, and found as left on him, tied at the
top, and sealed. In five minutes the ropes that had been
lashed about the man came over the other side to the
other committee; and, these being inspected, they were
not untied, the knots and twist remained the same, as
though the man had been taken out of them, and they had
dropped. In a few minutes I distinctly heard the box-lid
shut, not loud and heavy, but moderately and firmly. I
asked a lady beside me, "Did you hear that box shut?"
— "Yes, I did," she replied. I subsequently asked the
same question of others on the line of seats in front, and
received the same reply. In a few seconds a pistol was
discharged, as a signal that the feat was accomplished.

Instantly the curtains were drawn; and the man was found to be in the box, while the box was intact as it had been left, the lashing untouched. The ropes had been so thoroughly interlaced, that they could not be readily undone, and they were cut loose. The sheriff then took the key from his pocket, unlocked the irons, and opened the box; when the man jumped out, made his bow, and said, "Never was there, in all the exhibits and tyings of Spiritualism, any one tied closer or firmer than I have been to-night. The ropes have cut into my flesh. The feat would have been accomplished in ten minutes, had I not been so severely bound."

That spirits had assisted him, he did not conceal; but he left the spectators to draw their own conclusions as to how the work was done. In all probability there was not another of the spectators than myself who could tell how the wonder was accomplished. The bag and ropes were expanded, opened out, as it were, into the air, when they fell outside. The lashings and irons on the box expanded, loosened, that is, dematerialized, for the moment; then the man got into the box, and it closed on him intact. It must have done this, or I could not have heard it close. There was no other solution of the feat.

Several hundred persons could verify this statement, while perhaps thousands have seen it exhibited as legerdemain.

The performer was evidently one of the best kind of physical mediums, although ignoring the name for popularity's sake. As matter is clear, transparent, to spirits, they see its elements; and, if knowing how to use them, such feats are easily performed.

Question. — Why is it that clear and true statements are not given by those professing to give information as spirits?

Answer. — Because the instruments of earth are subjects of teachings and prejudice, and the spirits come under their conditions. Again, much is conveyed, even by those who are better informed, for the purpose of catering to the public appetite. The children of earth are not prepared to receive a full display of all that the spheres might convey; neither would they appreciate it if given. Spirits that have passed beyond the earth's conditions rarely use the organs of another.

The following lesson contained in " Flashes of Light " is *àpropos* to this theme, and gives a clear statement of the law : —

" Be it understood, that although enlightened spirits, upon all subjects, stand ready to give light to others, they are only suffered to impart in accordance with the law which controls them. When the benighted spirits ask in all honesty of soul for more light, and seek for it, are ready to receive it and make good use of it, then are they ready to give it. But, if it were forced upon the darkened spirit, the old maxim of earth would be applicable here, —

> ' The man convinced against his will
> Is of the same opinion still.'

" Spirits do not find that difficulty in overcoming their erroneous opinions that you may suppose. You should not think, that, because they do not jump into immediate knowledge after death, they have a hard time to attain it. But it is the law of all spirits, that they advance by slow and distinct degrees. There are no arches to span the gulfs over which spirits can march at will : they must ascend the ladder of human wisdom — no round being overlooked — ere they can pass out of darkness into light. The sun does not come immediately as the shades of night begin to disappear; and Nature moves in all her departments slowly and surely. Thus it is with spirit.''

This beautiful lesson shows that spirits through media can give only what is in their sphere of knowledge, and are not in possession of all knowledge of advanced lights.

Question. — Is the spirit-world, or spirit, the sphere of cause, or the sphere of effects?

Answer. — It is both cause and effect. A condition may exist in spirit as the effect of cause in the external life. Soul is cause: spirit is the effect, or result, of both. Therefore it is not absolutely true that spirit is all cause. The same law is true of the external world. It is both. It originates many causes that have an effect in spirit. Man and his intelligence is the effect of soul externalizing with matter and its conditions. This by some will be called the action of spirit on matter. How, then, can it be absolutely known that man is the result of one cause? Let it be understood that one condition depends on the other. When the two worlds are blended so intimately, do not think that one can exist without the other. It is a marriage of soul and matter: the offspring of the union is spirit.

TYPES AND RACES.

Perhaps there is no theme in science, theology, or theories, that has been so diversifiedly theorized as the genesis, development, and destiny of man and races. These are represented by a dozen different hypotheses coming down from a great, infinite God, or coming up from a mollusk or jelly-fish through animal life to the orang-outang into man.

We do not expect to deal with these self-poised sophists, but to give our own observations and the teachings of superior intelligences, and let humanity judge which is most conformable with reason. We hold that types are indestructible in nature ; that one type will not unite with another type to produce another kind, but will become extinct in external life first. We can not see that even birds which are of the same nature will promiscuate, but rather become solitary. The vegetable never evolved the organic being.

That many species of the same type exist both in animal and human is too well known to deny. We see this in the horse, the zebra, the ass, the many classes of goats, of canine, of fowls, and other typal creatures, up to the races of the human. These are but species of their types, and may commingle and bring out a mixed or improved species. But to affirm that one type is merged into some other is setting at defiance all analogy, and trampling on natural law as manifested to the lowest understanding.

Therefore there is but one human type, and five species. Ethnologists call them races. This raises the queries, What is species? What is race?

Species are a group of individuals or things that have an essential identity in qualities proceeding from their ultimate nature. Species are supposed to mingle and vary.

Race is a continued series of descent from a parent who is the first stock. A race can be of one kind : when it varies it runs out, or becomes a mixed race. The continued reproduction of one species has made the races : even allowing that a crossing of kind will produce a difference, there must be a first kind to make the cross. That the human species are not identical in kind, hardly requires showing : there is such a vast difference, physically, mentally, intellectually, in character and habits, that the differences will not harmonize.

One of the most difficult problems that the various

schools of theory find to handle is the origin of the different races. To solve this problem the most extravagant hypotheses are resorted to; giving climatic changes, diet, soil, habits, and what not. But the most novel is that of simulating man to a plant undergoing all the metamorphosis by transplanting and climatic changes. This might be answered, Yankee fashion, by asking a question: Tell us why the negro is the same to-day all over the earth? He has been perhaps two hundred years on the continent of America, and has not changed his skin, hair, features, nor character, to Indian or white. They have been over two hundred years in the West Indies and San Domingo; and there they retain African blackness and negro habits.

The Indian is indigenous to North America; and yet the descendants of the Pilgrim Fathers, after two centuries on the same continent, have shown no tendency to adopt the life and character of the Indian, while the poor Indian has given way, and is fast becoming extinct. Yet the American continent has had no great changes for the past three hundred years. You may make all the changes by "transplanting" or migration that it is possible to make with the same race, and yet they will produce no change in species. When it can be shown that a race has ever modified by climatic changes, it can be used as argument: until then, it is a chimera.

The Israelites of this time are a race because they rarely intermarry with other people. Now, they have lived and traveled in all countries, and have none of their own; and, wherever they are, they retain distinct features and characteristics distinguishing them from others. It is said, persistent habits or practices will produce a change in the transmittal to posterity, and a continual perseverance will ultimate in a different genus. This theory has no real basis of facts to rest upon, while there are numerous

examples to show that it will not apply to the human kind.
It is demonstrated facts that should sustain a theory, and
not hypothesis. As an illustration of fact open to all for
observation, we make the following statement. On the
north-west coast of America, from the Upper Columbia to
Puget Sound, there ranges a tribe of Indians called " Flat-
heads."

The name is derived from a practice they have of
flattening the heads of their females. It is done mechanically, with bark, stone, or hard wood, pressed on the
forehead of the newly-born female child ; and this is
continued until it has the desired shape, and the bones are
fixed. The process is kept up six or eight months, while
the head grows up high and flat, back and front ; thus
giving that high key to the arch of intelligence that many
persons claim to be an indication of future superiority.
It appears as though it was done to enable these dragging,
overburdened women to carry their burdens with more
facility ; for they are beasts of toil from the age of ten
years. These Indians have practiced this form of alteration several hundred years, and to this day there is not
one that has brought forth a flat-headed child. Here are .
mothers, prolific, whose physical structure is altered in
the most phrenological sense, who are seeing the alteration
continually before their eyes, if a female is present from
one day old to a hundred years ; yet there is no change of
germs or gemmules conveyed to the form of their offspring, and they are compelled to keep up the rites
mechanically.

A practice of the Chinese is another example. This
nation, or race, shave the heads of their males as soon as
the hair grows an inch long, leaving a patch on the crown
the size of the hand, from which depends the cue. This
they have practiced three thousand years : yet Nature,

as if in defiance of their perseverance, persists in growing on their heads a coarse, thick, black hair, which they must shave every week through their lives to keep the head bare. By this time they should be a race of bald-heads, if habits or continued practices could effect a change in germs, or natural law could be deviated.

Then the Israelites, who are so scrupulous to marry with their own race, have practiced the rite of circumcision three thousand years; and yet there is not a deviation in their offspring from the order of germs of their own nature. This shows that habits and practices continued for many ages have produced no change from the primitive stock. When such long, persistent practices have had no effect on these three races, can it be consistent with reason to suppose that one race will change to another by the action of soil and climate? or that the white race is the result of a transplanting of the negro, evolving gradually to the blonde? O Consistency! what a jewel thou art when set in the forehead of those who pretend to teach others!

In contrast with such a variety of scientific lore, I give what supernal intelligence conveys.

Question. — How, in the beginning, did human beings take up their abode on earth?

Answer. — In the beginning, the earth moved in the ethereal spirit-matter; and germs of the human, like the rest, moved in ethereal space.

The human descent was of the ethereal nature of spirit. In the earliest states of the earth, vegetable first developed, then animal. When the earth was sufficiently developed, man in the original took up his abode on it from other spheres, as a distinct type and species: these became more and more material. Therefore man was an original descent of spirit, not of the higher intelligence, but of an inferior grade, with low, gross, animal instincts. As spirit does not lose its instincts, these in time pro-created, and man became an established, incarnate being. Man has not changed in the aggregate ; but his intelligence has advanced as he developed, being first subject to the crude and undeveloped conditions of those early epochs. The human shape has been so many countless cycles in its resemblance, that intelligence can not trace its origin. Other worlds that have been created, and run their course as this, have passed away ; and the germs of similarity came in this way. Races are as distinctive creations as any one species of animal life. They are not derived from one kind, but have come on the earth, each by itself, to its own section, where they multiplied. The law of natural selection is well enough in its kind, and as a means of improving species ; but it can not apply to the change of types, nor to the propagating and bringing forth of the human kind. There has been a difference that can not be reconciled by any such theory. It is true, there have been differences in growth and development ; that giants and dwarfs have existed : but they are the exceptions. The earth has never been inhabited by mas-todons and giants as a distinctive feature, though there have been individual instances of such creations. If it is borne in mind that the earth is but a speck in the uni-verse, and that other spheres are represented by the same human kind, even into far-distant spheres, and the past ages show the same, how can it be said mankind in stature or shape are an evolvement from the brute, or came from one pair?

The earth, therefore, has been peopled by the power of spirit. Soul here has shown its instinctive force, and universal law its action. This law is, that all space is filled with matter, soul, spirit, creative germs, and

solar magnetic force. An inter-exchange is received, and
spheres are continually thrown off, some in more advanced
development than others. In this way there passes a
germinal principle to new and developing planets, and a
ceaseless succession or rotation is going on throughout the
universe. The action of this law can not be better seen
than in the pollen of plants that are conveyed any distance, while their derivation is not known, but, when the
elements are adaptable, will germinate.

Each race or species on the earth is original of its kind,
and took its sectional divisions where they are found, and
multiplied. The negro is supposed to be the most primitive, as he is the next removed from the animal type;
the Indian next; the Malay is of the same generic kind,
and the same advent; the Mongolian or Asiatic is the
first approach to the white race; the Caucasian, as the
white, is the Northman of Europe and Central Asia.
These races remain the same in kind, if not amalgamated.
They never would change physically in their generating
by location or climatation. Nature will maintain her laws.
The Egyptians were a class of Ethiopians and Malays,
with Asiatics, that miscegenated, and proved themselves
adepts; the Malays and Asians migrating to that section.
Their antiquity approximates twelve or fifteen thousand
years. Other inferior species, the Australian, Patagonian,
South-sea-Islander, are of the same generic kind as the
African. Their location is determined by the change in
the configurations of the earth's surface by the convulsions
of past ages.

The divine law of creation could not be improved on
when seen in its grand total, its great economy, and its
serial progressive movements. In nothing is it better
exhibited than in the adaptation of the various races of
mankind to the conditions and stages of the soul's progress externalizing in lower forms.

Question. — I have seen it stated that germs of being were of each species contained in the elements of the earth, and that the germs of the human being were of the organic elements of the globe. How does it compare with facts?

Answer. — There is no such thing as independent priority of earth's elements: it partakes of what is common to the universe. Call it matter, ether, fluids, liquid substances, or protoplasm: these are scientific names for one principle, and are used indiscriminately to mean creative essences. All space is filled with ethereal matter carrying germs of life. When a planet has attained a stage of development in which it can sustain animal life, such will be attracted to it as can sustain themselves and develop. In this way the primitive organic beings found a lodgement, and prepared the way for the races.

Question. — Is this called spontaneous development?

Answer. — Spontaneous growth of organic beings never did take place on earth, or on any other sphere, without soul and the intervention of spirit-essences. As before stated, soul, matter, and spirit-essences form a trinity of creative power.

Question. — What definition does spirit give to matter?

Answer. — Matter is the essential ether that fills space, serviceable to spirit as well as external life. Spirit acts through matter as well as organic life. Matter holds in solution all elements of organic life, all elements of gross substances, and all things whatsoever found in universal space ; and is at the service of spirit that has learned to utilize it.

RE-INCARNATION, OR SOUL'S TAKING FORM.

The doctrine of re-incarnation is not supposed to be acceptable to the English-reading people. Perhaps there

is no class that would abhor it as much as the Christian-
theology believers. Yet they are as near the truth as
most of the independent free-thinkers and spiritualists,
who prefer to say man has a very exalted origin or derivation, and give no more reasonable account for discre-
pancies than the others. To no class do we cater, nor
attempt to show favor. Popular sentiment will be antagonistic, generally. But truth against the world shall pre-
vail. It is for time that we write, let the present gen-
eration think as it may. It is not a question of likes and
dislikes, when truth is in the balance-scale. What should
be of more interest to humanity than to know the purposes
and uses of life, and the principle that actuates all?

The subject as here treated is little, if any, understood
by man on earth; and much less is he willing to receive
or understand it. Nevertheless, it is a law in action that
can not be evaded; and all that are intelligent enough to
read these lines have experienced it, and have gathered
the benefits of that experience.

Soul, in its first taking animated form, clothes itself
with the simplest form of animal life. In that form it
learns of the elements; and, in contact with crude, gross
matter, the instinct is manifested, and this in accordance
with the physical form, or the law of matter it exercises.
And when, by the law of cause and effect, life is ejected
from that form, it is only released from disintegrating,
gross matter. With what knowledge it has gained of material and the external world, the same principle remains,
to take another round in some higher form, it may be but
a step in advance. In time, the same law disinthralls
from the second standard: and, so on, these advances are
made from one to a grade higher; and, as each passage is
made, it gains in knowledge and perception of eternal
things.

Reptiles and fishes are not included in this category: these belong to the elements, and Nature's law of matter. But the feathered family are moved and controlled by soul-principle.

It does not follow, that, when one form is cast off, another is taken on immediately; for more or less time intervenes. In the more advanced stages, there is a rest of centuries. The soul clothes itself with form through the external world of matter; and, when the life principle that has animated it is released, it is seen in spirit in a form like that it has occupied on earth. In time those elements of spirit-matter are dispersed, and it loses all the conditions of that individual form, and the principle is free in space. The intelligent part is taken up, and utilized to some higher form: this is done by the action of its own law, moved as well by Nature's law. Every thing is governed by natural law: you can not transcend or go beyond it. Soul, or intelligence, can only act through this same law, infinite in its operation. As shown in preceding pages, all intelligence can not be gained at one term. The soul is not equal to human expression, until, refined by the power of spirit-conditions, it loses its antecedent earthly nature, retaining only the intelligent; and, when this is sufficient to fill human form, it is moved in that direction.

When a soul takes up its abode in the human, it is not then qualified for the higher development, but must first learn the use and nature of the human senses, the practicality of its form, and all the primary requisites of human life. Some of these manifestations are very crude; others, that have better associations, have that much advantage. The soul will not in its initial step take human form only in the lowest, but after that may take any of the more advanced. The very lowest human species is the negro in his native state, and the first removed from animal life. In the millions of years they have been on the earth, they have not within themselves developed to any appreciable extent, and, if left to themselves, would return to their original condition. When the negro enters spirit-life he is in the position which his intelligence entitles him to, the same as all others : but the same law acts upon him, and causes him to feel he is not equal to the situation ; and in time his special individuality is lost, and he rests, to take another round when the time comes.

This does not imply that a negro, or inferior race, becomes extinct in the spirit-world : for that there is a continual motion and renewal in this or some other sphere is inevitable. No species is lost.

In this way the soul seeks its highest attainment in form, and intelligent knowledge of the external, material world. Until this is attained, there will be a repeated taking of form.

Question. — Will not some minds say that all this can be as well accomplished in spirit-life as it can by adopting this formula?

Answer. — Let it be remembered, you are always virtually in the position of soul ; and it is only the change of conditions from one state to another, in which matter is only an incidental means by which to manifest ; and that you are doing this even in the short term of one life, with a constant aspiration for something more.

Question. — But why does not the spirit retain and carry with it a knowledge of all these passages and experiences?

Answer. — Simply from the fact, that, when the soul is changing its conditions, there is a desire to leave its individuality, the detail of the external. Sometimes this assumes an intense desire to take another course. The intelligence is all that is sought for : this the spirit draws from, and thus makes a practical use of its past experiences. If this were not done, mankind would be in a state of savagery to this time ; whereas, as it now is, their progress is exemplified in the mental activity and ceaseless aspiration for more, with an intuitive idea of the spiritual. The soul does not retain a knowledge of past earthly life, because there is no desire to remember it.

Question. — The spirit, then, as an intelligence, has not existed for all time?

Answer. — The spirit in that light has not ; only as soul, which may be designated as spirit if it suits best. Many people make no distinction, and do not know the difference between spirit-essences and intelligent soul. A soul, being a unit in the universe of souls, has the property, common to each, to move with instinctive force. In this light it is that there is a principle in human nature without beginning and without end. While the conditions change, the identity remains. In regard to our past career, of which the human family is so tenacious, preferring to believe they descend from some great " deific mind," or maybe fallen angels, let them once look around, and, seeing the great diversity of expressions and intellectual standings, consider whether it is reasonable to suppose a descent direct from one " deific mind."

What cares the man of science through what channel he gains his information, if the object is attained? The object for him to experiment with is as good in the Hottentot as it would be in a prince of full blood. No searcher after knowledge will reject the same because he has to search in the rudiments and first principles to find what he desires ; for he knows it must be done to have a thorough understanding of his subject. Does not the horticulturist delve in earth and guano in order to bring out the rarest and most beautiful flowers? The same rule is applicable here. The channel through which it comes is of no consequence to the operator : the attainment is all-essential.

Question. — The spiritualists claim that knowledge and progress come through spirit-conditions, and that all advance is made from a spiritual stand-point.

Answer. — That is true only to some extent. There must be capacity for it : where there is an aspiration, a seeking and desire, such will be conveyed. But there is a great diversity of mind and intellect. Some are not perceptive, while others would not make the knowledge serviceable if conveyed. There must be a capacity to receive and utilize what is given.

Spiritualists are receiving many progressive ideas ; but the ages have been preparing mankind for them. Time has not been without its results upon the present denizens of earth. Through them the people have come up to their present receptive condition ; and yet they are not capable of receiving all that can be conveyed to them, and what future ages will receive.

Question. — What is the process through which the spirit makes this change? How is the spirit conscious of it?

Answer. — The entering spirit-life is only a change of location : the personal characteristics remain the same. When a spirit has not the required knowledge for the position in which he is placed, but little advance is made, and he may hold his position near the earth for one year to a century : but in time he will lose strength ; he will feel his incapacity and deficiency for spirit-conditions : then a weariness, an exhaustion, comes over him, and the light grows less, a torpor supervenes, and he rests in space an allotted time. He is only conscious of his weakness, and that he is not adapted to the sphere in which he is.

When the time of repose is accomplished, a restlessness shows itself, betraying a semi-conscious state ; then there is some special principle that guides and controls, that leads to the channel of his desires. In very many instances the force and condition of parentage attract, and this instinct of attraction leads to the desired object.

Question. — Is there any special allotment for individual souls?

Answer. — In some instances there is. Some may have had special desires, some an extended experience, while others have nothing special.

Question. — What has the moral character to do with re-incarnation? Has it any bearing on the subject?

Answer. — The moral character has something to do with it in a special sense ; but in a general sense it has not. A person may be moral in his own own light, while to another he would be quite immoral.

When a person is on a low animal plane, vicious and brutish, the moral character shows a low, degraded nature : this would have bearing on his re-incarnation, because such a one would be unsuited in the spheres to bear the memory of his previous career. Morality is judged differently by the laws of spirit and the laws made by man. The soul judges itself by the power it has had to know right from wrong. A person may be intelligent and immoral knowingly : such suffers severely the torments of memory for evil-doing, and would gladly accept oblivion, if possible, to escape the pangs of memory. The worst sin a human being can be guilty of is that of causing his fellow-man suffering and want.

Licentiousness and fornication are causes of great sorrow to the spirit ; but onanism is the unpardonable sin, and, if persisted in, befogs the spirit.

Drunkenness is also a severe affliction to the spirit ; and, as it entails so many other evils, it makes the drunkard's position almost unbearable. These are the immoral habits that most affect the spirit, and entail regrets, if not suffering, as long as memory lasts. Therefore many would be glad to make the change, to rest, and take up another career, if they could.

Question. — What relation does the suicide bear to the subject?

Answer. — The suicide is never such, in fact: he has only changed his field of action to another; and, if he does it to escape trouble, he has only added to it; for it is better that life should reach its full length.

Question. — Can the friends of these resting souls know how they are conditioned, or trace them in subsequent time?

Answer. — Each and every soul is traceable through its conditions. But the immediate friends may not be able to do this until they have advanced to that stage of being where they are fitted for it. All soul has a union in essence : there is a common interest in its expression. When one enters the spirit-spheres, there remain the memory, attractions, and affections of earthly associations ; but, as time elapses, these attractions lessen, and they enter more fully the conditions of spirit. Then the relationship is not looked upon the same : it is not so exclusive, and they bear a common interest with others.

Question. — Are these resting souls what are called dark, vicious spirits? Do they have any influence on those of earth?

Answer. — These are not represented in that light. They could not be vicious, tormenting ; nor can they cast any influence on those of earth, their condition being one of torpor. The dark spirits are a totally different class. There are likewise other resting spirits not of this condition.

Question. — Why is it that some spirits have not given to us some correct idea on this subject, while others positively deny it?

Answer. — From the fact that they are not acquainted with it, and are not developed to comprehend it. It is only intelligences of advanced light that see it, and these can not fully comprehend the manifesting of soul. It is hid within itself, yet is governed by law. We are not in possession of infinite powers, and find none that are. We are learning as we advance.

Under-grades of spirits may know there is such a law; but of its workings they know not.

When the world learns that the spirit state is a progressive one, they will believe that all knowledge is not in possession of the latest arrivals.

Sex. — There being no sex to soul-principle, it, like form, is developed by Nature's process, the distinction she carries out for procreating. It is the distinguishing feature of the germ in its inception : therefore germs have the character of the sex as it has the type. The soul takes no cognizance of sex in its original, but may take either form from one time to another. In time it finds a decided cast, and remains such in spirit. The last is the most important to us, and all we need care for, or that spirit has interest in.

FETAL LIFE AND GENERATING.

Question. — At what time does the soul take possession of the form, — at conception, or at birth?

Answer. — At the moment of time it draws the first breath, when it comes in contact with the atmosphere ; not while in the matrice. There is a law of generating in itself.

Question. — Why is it that most statements of spirits have been, that it was at the moment of conception?

Answer. — Such statements come from those who have been educated to consider it so. It is the old religious theory they remember. While ignorant of the law and the facts, they promulgate a dogma ingrafted by inheritance. But the time that a child is conceived is *not* the time it can be moved by human soul.

Question. — Will you be so kind as to give the laws of generating?

Answer. — The conditions of generating are in the mother. She holds the power to attract, retain, and throw off. When the elements are blended, the process is not dissimilar to that of the seed sown in the ground. It is nurtured and brings forth in the same manner, and is purely a reproduction of kind. The seed of the woman receives the male elements ; then it takes root in her matrice, grows like its parent stock, and draws its nutriment the same as the fruit from the tree. In time, the magnetic flow from the mother gives the motion ; and the currents of electric life-forces from the mother are the moving power, as well as the sustaining of its embryo. In the matrice the embryo has no functions : there are no lungs that act, no brain that is sensitive ; the heart itself does not move as in external life ; but these are forming, growing as instruments of use when made.

The parent, then, is the whole life-force : her electric and magnetic elements as well as substances propel and influence the embryo in its physical organism, compelling it to be like its parent stock.

There is no established spirit while *in utero :* while dependent on the mother it may die, and nothing would result from it except a waste of matter. As a tumor of her own substance is thrown off; as a tree sends out shoots that would not live without sap from their parent source, and are equally useless when cut off : even so the growth of

an embryo is the bearing of fruit, and has no other relation to spirit-life.

The atmosphere is a vitalizing element in nature, that
gives action and force to matter. The embryo having
grown with organs to sustain life, Nature asserts her law,
like the fruit, that, when ripe, the tree allows to fall, and it
comes forth into its new element. The functions are started
by the lungs drawing in air and vitality, propelling sensation to the brain, and starting the currents of life in their
proper channels. Soul-principle is present by the attractive force of conditions; and this new form is now a quick-
ened soul, able to live independently if properly nourished.
This is the law and conditions of generating.

Let us analyze the theory promulgated by those who
insist upon the conception of spirit. In order to do this,
the theory asserted should be understood. Let it be asked
of such theorist, What is the principle conveyed, and
how? what its actions or movements? Does it exclusively
belong to one parent to give it? or is it a supernatural
action? If it is conveyed by either parent, then they are
the creators of their offspring, and there is no principle
in humanity antecedent to conception.

If it is a supernatural action, there must be some special
divine attention given at the time to the act of cohabiting.
How can this be attributed to a personal God? Such theorists must acknowledge the universal God of Nature, if
they would evade the first dilemma. This they will not do.
The theory implies that there is virtually a soul, perhaps
two or three, in the woman's form, aggregating to themselves elemental matter to take forms. If such could be
the fact, what should be the state of that woman? It
should be one of extraordinary strength, mental and physical activity, when her body is the lodging-place of several
of the "divine emanations." But the reverse of this is

true. All well know that gestation is a fatiguing, exhaustive state, with more or less nervous mental depression, and perhaps physical derangement, showing that it is purely the result of a multiplication and division of her forces.

Some prefer to adopt the monad theory, — that the male at puberty inhales monads, and, entering the circulation, they pass through all the organs, and so on into spermatozoa; that these monads are repelled from female magnetisms, the female not imbibing them, — giving to male the exclusive creative power, the conveying of soul or spirit. In regard to this theory, it is all man, the lord of creation.

Monad truth is this: It is well known that the atmosphere is freighted with animal and vegetable life. Monads are animalcules floating in the air; and, breathed, they enter the circulation, and the blood is vitalized with animalcule life. There is decomposition, and it passes off sooner or later. This is not peculiar to one sex, kind, or animal: all that breathe take in alike.

But these monads are not soul-germs: they have no power or principle to receive intelligence. They are simply the result of decomposing animal matter. We imbibe them in sickness and contagion in the atmosphere as septic germs. · Therefore there are no soul-monads for males to imbibe.

The male engenders spermatozoa for procreative purposes, which, in consort with the ovum, generate their kind. The ovum is the substance and matter to afford nutriment, while the spermatozoa quicken with magnetic force and generative strength. The two elements blended create a germ of their own kind: let it germinate, or be lost, it is one. Generating, then, is an animal function carried on by natural laws without divine or supernatural intervention. When the form is adapted for it, soul or spirit takes possession by obsession of this new matter, and grows in external life with it. To show that I am not alone in the position I take, I here give an item from "The Voice of Angels," from Swedenborg, through a medium, Dr. Dexter, entitled "Body and Soul: " —

"The spirit which enters the body of the child, on being born, is the principle, or germ. The soul enters a body the moment that body requires natural mortality, or life. It grows with the body, and assumes its shape, form, appearance, and sex. The development of the body, either male or female, determines the sex of the soul; for, when it emanates from the source as a principle, it has no sex; and, though we pass through many transformations after birth, the soul always maintains its sex in whatever state it may exist."

Reading this item, I telegraphed to Swedenborg to know how he understood this application. He replied, —

"I do not understand there is any sentient principle in the womb. I do not consider there is soul in the embryo while sustained by the mother principle : there is being forming ; but I consider in that respect the parent is the creator of the offspring. By natural mortality, or life, I mean independent existence from parent form. Then it is that soul enters external life, and is in sentient form."

These ideas correspond with the teachings throughout this work, and are in direct reversal of the other theory, that soul is conceived and has being in the parent womb. Thus, we maintain, the parent creates that form from its own elements, physically and mentally ; and the soul has to operate with this material and its predisposition. It is a duality, a marriage of matter and soul for external life. It does not seem as though further demonstration of our position could be required, it is so comprehensive : if more is required, I refer then to the passage on duality.

From all our showing, it is evident that man is in the image of God simply because he holds all the elements, physically and mentally, existing in the universe, either developed or attainable. He is a microcosm of all beneath him, and will ascend to all above him. Thus he is in the image of Nature's God, and not of God as a personal being.

CHILDHOOD AS SPIRIT.

Question. — Does the child develop physically and intellectually in spirit as it would on earth?

Answer. — It does not. The child enters spirit as the child : the object and purposes of its being have not been accomplished ; the laws of physical life have not been fulfilled. There is no influx of superior power because it has become spirit. Childhood is innocent and dependent. Children have no cares, and no responsibility. They are joyous and happy, and home and parents are their greatest attractions. When they enter spirit-life these connections are the greatest remembrances to them, and for a time they are supposed to be familiar with them. These things in time change, lose in interest and strength ; and the child rests from time to time until it takes a long rest, after which the same results follow with them as with other souls. But this rest is not so protracted with the young as those of more mature years.

Question. — How long may a child remain in spirit before it is exhausted?

Answer. — That depends on the age and strength of the child. From three or six years to fifty and more.

Question. — Do children manifest and show the memory they have of earth by returning?

Answer. — They most certainly do, and to a great extent, because they are associated with the earthly conditions of their parents ; and this will continue so long as the parents' condition calls it out. There is an exchange of currents between the parent and the child even into the spirit-life ; and, so long as this has force, the child will be more or less conditioned by it. But these must necessarily weaken with time.

Question. — At what age is there sufficient development for continued spirit-life?

Answer. — That depends wholly on the ability of the child.

Question. — How is it, or why is it, that fully-matured minds, materialized forms, come and represent to us that they entered the spirit-world as infant-children, but now show themselves in full stature, claiming relationship, etc.?

Answer. — That is something that never was genuine : it is deception, practiced by designing spirits who wish to make an exhibit. No infant could return grown to full stature during the life on earth of its parent. Childhood's advance in spirit is slower than that would allow ; and they are not possessed of elements sufficient to form statures they never had. The infant is not an infant, in fact, unless it has a consciousness of itself. When childhood is in spirit, it is attached to the elements of its parents and the recollections of its short life ; but then it does not follow that they are developed to statures beyond what they had attained in external life. They are like plants taken from the earth, that wilt unless replanted : they will not bloom, bear fruit, nor shed the seeds of maturity.

Facts within the knowledge of the writer, bearing on this theme, may here be given.

Some years ago, a medium in trance persisted in representing to me a statement from two children claiming to be my girl and boy, grown up in spirit-life, who wished to let me know of themselves; whereas the facts are, I never lost a child at any stage of growth, from conception to the present time.

In the summer of 1875 a man called to see me. His wife had been in spirit thirteen years. They had buried three children prior to her own death; one a boy of nine years. She came to him, and gave communications, and spoke of their grown-up family and married children. This led him to inquire for those in spirit. Then she said, "I have not found them." This he expressed as appearing remarkable to him; for she had made that same statement before through a trance-medium in Oregon; and to hear it thus repeated surprised him.

My mother, with whom I have been as familiar in spirit as when on earth, and much more confidential, buried three infants, — one of three months, one still-born, and the third eighteen months, — all of them in spirit, approximately, forty years; certainly long enough to attain to some stature, according to the views of writers. When she had been in spirit three years, I asked about her infants. She replied, "I have not found them, and do not expect to. I hope their little souls will have better opportunities when nurtured by some other mother." My father, who followed them into spirit only one year after the last, never obtained any information of them; while their sister on earth, who has been most familiar with all the relations and friends who have passed to spirit in the past fifty years, has never had the remotest intimation of their whereabouts. Forty years, and not heard from! Under these circumstances we may ask, Can these be exceptions to the general law of life? The plain truth is, they enter spirit-life with little consciousness of earth, and so remain; and this is the general law of infants, notwithstanding the assertions of nearly all theorists to the contrary.

The tenets of this dogma are, *First*, that spirit is conveyed at conception; that at any time after conception, let it be days, weeks, or months, if the germ in embryo is lost, that germ is carried away as waste matter; but the spirit lives in spirit-life, develops to full stature and mental advancement, the same as though material life had been its experience. *Second*, That infancy and childhood are subject to like conditions; "that, remaining near the earth, they draw of its elements and material to grow in stature precisely the same as they would had they remained on earth to mature age." These dogmas are equivalent to saying, man is the whole originator of his being; and the spirit-world is being peopled to a great extent from embryonic germs that had no external life. Such are represented to be in spirit, pure and ethereal in form, angelic in looks and fact. If such is the true result from entering spirit without any appreciable materiality, then it is not essential for mankind to live to maturity and old age; for by so doing they acquire bad habits, vices, and evil propensities accompany them, for which they are responsible: whereas, if they nearly all died young, they would escape these evils, and be pure spirit in form and intellect, and the spirit-world would be more perfect, less temptations exist to those on earth, and both spheres be benefited thereby. Such theories — and they are extensively promulgated from every rostrum — make it questionable how it could be intended for man's good to experience the life on earth.

The position held in these pages is, life has a purpose to fulfill in external being, and this purpose can not be evaded; that soul carries with it the demands of its fulfillment, and executes it without so much as saying, "By your leave, my Lord." To show I am sustained by well-informed spirit authority, I give an extract from Judd

Pardee, taken from "The Voice of Angels." He says,
" Life on the lower plane is positively necessary for development and unfoldment of the human soul out of darkness.   All things animate or inanimate, whether they
relate to the lower or higher kingdoms, take their starting-
point in the womb of darkness ; and the very lowest conditions are necessary before it is possible for higher ones
to exist."

Here, in these few words, is a confirmation of the
whole platform these pages rest upon.   Who could ask
more ?   Where are the " Gods," " Divine minds,"
" Over-souls," and " Essences, " from whom man emanates, according to the views of many?   Let Swedenborg,
Pardee, the prompters of these pages, and others, seek
them out ; for have not superior minds on earth asserted
such exist?

DEMONSTRATED ILLUSTRATIONS ON RE-INCARNATION.

From the preceding chapters, it must be evident that
childhood and infancy do not impress on its subsequent
form or organism the detail of former being.   When
there is little experience, there is nothing to remember.
This is an all-sufficient proof that minds are not conscious
of it in the external.   The soul can not exercise govern-
mental power in two spheres at the same time.   External
life is burdensome all through, and so oppressed with its
cares that little else is thought of.   When these burdensome cares are done with, there is a more interior spirit-
part ; and, if there has been an antecedent experience im-
pressed on the spirit, it is likely to be indistinctly recalled.
This accounts for the statements some spirits make respecting themselves.   For instance, I had an intimate
friend, who when on earth was a doctor, a man of worth,
and the best of morals.   He has been in spirit ten years.

He says, that, soon after entering spirit-life, he remembered his former existence; that he was of the Hebrew race, a boy of eighteen or twenty years, and he thought that he well remembered a field he had something to do with. His statement was truthful, taking in consideration the occasion of his making it. It would have been detected if untrue.

One who had been in spirit-life nearly two thousand years, and who when on earth was known as a teacher and reformer, has stated that he distinctly remembered while on earth that he had filled some other condition prior to the one he then occupied, and, when advanced in spirit, learned that he had been of an entirely different race.

Here I must introduce the reader to something relating more to the external realities of life.

In January, 1876, a circle of spirits gathered in my humble dwelling at regular intervals, until a large number were accustomed to be present. The object was sociability, instruction, and development. Among them were several bright and well-advanced spirits; one an old Indian, and a leader in this gathering. He had been two thousand years in spirit-life, and his name was Cenis. He was represented by others as being a well-developed intelligence, and an excellent psychometrist and soul-tracer; evidence of the truth of which will be shown in the recital of transactions at this gathering, which lasted three weeks. During this time some vivid as well as extraordinary demonstrations were made on this subject, which will explain themselves best in their narration, and show the reality, and in some instances the manner, of its operation. The manifestations at this circle necessitate my giving some knowledge I had of the characters while they were on earth.

Some years ago I lived in the house with a blind girl, one whose eyes had been pierced in an operation for cataract at the age of ten years. When I knew her, she was seventeen; and I took much interest in her, and sought to benefit her. After I left the place, I never saw her again. She was an only child; and her mother allowed her free association with all, and liberty to do as she desired. The mother was a free-and-easy kind of person: so a great many gentlemen visited her blind daughter, ostensibly out of sympathy, as she was interesting, cheerful, and gay. In time she married; not, however, until she was with child, and the marriage became compulsory.

I did not know that any of them were in spirit-life until at this circle the mother and step-father made their appearance among us with this daughter, a pitiable object, shocking all the sensibilities of those present to behold.

They gave an account of and identified themselves to me thoroughly; but their burden was their unfortunate child, for whose condition the mother was freely and liberally censured by the whole circle. The daughter, Nette, was brought in contact with my elements to establish her memory as best she could, and externalize her experiences: after this she gave an account of herself, relating some of her unfortunate experiences.

Her mother rented lodging-rooms in her house: she gave the girl an upper room to herself, on the floor where every other room was occupied by male lodgers. Under these circumstances access was gained to her by a young man, who introduced to her the most shocking practices known to humanity below the brute. With the details I will not pollute these pages. They are unmentionable, and without name. The man I knew; and for this reason I was given a more minute account of her initiation into what became a habit, and made her a total human wreck.

This led to lewdness with others. After her marriage she was little better in habits until she became monomaniac in her horrible taste. This was the first knowledge her mother had of her habit, when it was shown to her tangibly. From this state she became imbecile, and a disgust to the man she married, who could not support her presence. She had children : this they desired to stop, from which efforts she was badly injured : this necessitated Cesarean operation to take away a seven-months child. The wound never healed ; and she lingered, not able to put her feet on the floor, a year, and then died, aged twenty-eight years. Her frightful state was such a shock and grief to her mother, it affected her health : she went into decline, and died very soon after.

As she was censured for neglect of watchful care over her child in the beginning, she said, " I never thought of such a thing. She was blind, and I did not wish to deprive her of any of the pleasures she could have in life : and I thought she was pleased to have the attention of men ; and, to gratify her, I let her have all the freedom she chose."

Thus this woman's conception of the greatest pleasure of life to a blind girl was masculine freedom. The results were, she had no mental nor moral culture ; no knowledge of the world ; and all her intellect ran in the groove of the worst animal passions, producing imbecility. In spirit she was chained, as it were, to the mother, who was not permitted to be a moment without her. It had been her punishment to be on the move from circle to circle among the spirits, exhibiting her burden and its frightful conditions ; to receive censure, then move on to some other : this way it had been with them for several years, when they unexpectedly found themselves in our midst, and before one yet on earth who had known them. The girl

was taken from the mother, and placed to rest in the care
of a matronly spirit for the time being, until further developments; and things remained in a quiescent state for
several days in regard to her.

The following character is nearer to me; being a cousin,
with whom I had some experience during the last few years.
This boy had all the advantages that schooling and money
could give. His father was a man of taste and means,
amply able and willing to do well by him. But the boy
was unmanageable, self-willed, reckless, and engaged in
every manner of mischief to give trouble. Seeing the
danger to his younger boys, the father sent him to a
Jesuit college in Canada. There the boy became so wild
and reckless in his deportment, that the college could not
keep him; and he was expelled. Then he made his way to
some friends, who shipped him to the Pacific coast, where
I first saw him, he being then in his seventeenth year. I
found him a singular-looking young man, with a face whose
expression was that of low cunning and viciousness, and
in which could be read bad character and revenge.

As he took his liberty from his custodians, I took interest in him, and became well acquainted with his ways and
nature. I found him more strange in character than in
appearance, and of a nature the most grotesque and per-
verse I ever knew. His education was better then than the
common average. He was apt and quick at perception;
and this he applied only to bad purposes. He was wild,
fractious, without stability, and addicted to every vice
known, not excepting one; while onanism was his habitual
practice. He would resort to the most unusual and un-
heard-of means to gain a point: full of conceit, angulari-
ties, and sharp points, he made himself a nuisance to every
one he came near. After being on the west coast a year,
he made his way back to his home and parents, by no

means the better for his absence. His father, fearing his contaminating influence on his brothers, and for other reasons, locked him in his room, and kept the key himself. This displeased him so much, he thought he would kill his father when he came to his door, and made preparations to do so ; but, having to wait some time, he became impatient, and turned his mind to himself, and determined he would do something that would give his friends trouble. So he fixed his gun to the door-key, and put a bullet through his brain, thus ending his career on earth in his nineteenth year.

Six months or more after his exit from earth-life, he made his appearance in my room; while other spirits of his connections were present, among them his aunt. His manner and deportment were as natural as it was possible to be, — full of antics, glee, and animation ; while he gave the most minute account of his manner of suicide, in which he expressed great satisfaction. To obtain his recital, the spirits questioned him closely in regard to how he manipulated his weapon. After this he showed how he acted when he saw with delight what he had done, — how he looked at the body, and danced for joy. His aunt asked why his father confined him. "Oh! because I played." This was in allusion to his habits. Then his aunt asked him how he was then employed? "I am exhibiting in one of the beer-cellars on Kearney Street, in 'Frisco," was his reply. This had been one of his places of resort while in earthly form. He at the same time related minutely his transactions with me.

All this time he did not address any thing to me, but wholly to the spirits who drew his attention. When Cenis said, " Let me show what you are, young man," he was horrified, begged to be excused, and skulked to one corner of the room ; after which he soon left.

I heard no more of him for six or seven montas; when he came to this circle, looking for his aunt. He begged for food, saying he was starving to death, and faint for nourishment, which he wanted her to furnish to him. This was all he said. Thus in one year, or a little more, he was exhausted and famishing for spirit nutriment; and was not able to sustain himself in spirit-life, even in his sphere. He weakened from a want of adaptability in his own forces.

There was not power in himself to draw pabulum that he could live by. He was like a fish out of its element, soon exhausted.

Shortly after his arrival in this august assemblage of spirits, intelligences from afar were heard to say, " Rest, rest! Cenis, rest the boy: such a one cannot make his way, nor travel to the sun."

Then followed electrical coruscations, giving a message written in the air so rapid I could not read it; but Cenis could. It said, " Rest eighteen hundred and twelve years." Again the coruscations, and the voice said, " Rest to Nette, eighteen hundred and twenty years."

Then Cenis proceeded to make passes as we would to magnetize one to sleep, calling on a matron present to assist him. The girl's mother gave out the most heartfelt and tearful exclamations of prayer and thanksgiving, saying, " Darling, darling Nette! you are blessed, blessed at last! Rest, unfortunate child, that you may be blessed. What a mercy in the Infinite Power to provide such a boon to afflicted humanity! It is not in my power to express my thanks: my heart is too full." Then she said, " We have been told we would find a circle at which she would be rested, but not when, nor how; and I never could have thought of its being at Mrs. K——'s."

This woman was deeply moved; for the whole circle

could feel it. After this, although she remained, she never spoke.

Let it here be understood this " rest " is not forced, nor made by the powers beyond. It is the inert weakness of the spirit soul itself, that can not draw pabulum from spirit-forces, nor recuperate from earth's conditions, that necessitate it.

The idea of a higher spirit manipulating is simply to give equipoise, and shed a ray of future light and force. The giving of a fixed time was only to convey to the circle some idea of a period of rest approximating to that number of years. The pneumatography shown in flashes of light came from superior spheres sending to the circle its light. After that, general interest was taken in the subject, and Cenis was solicited by those present to trace the antecedents of some of them. The matron he began with, saying, "There you are, W——, an Atlanten, a boy of nine years old, two thousand three years past." — " Well," she said, " I might expect that : I thought I had male elements always ; but what kind of animals were Atlantens? "—" They were not animals, but people whose descendants remained in Central America and Mexico after their continent was sunk." Then Cenis said, " I can trace you through quite plainly." — " Oh, no ! don't ! I'd rather not have you do so ; take some other one," she replied. This person was of marked characteristics on earth, of great force and executive ability ; totally different, mentally and physically, from her ancestors.

Several others were traced ; one to the old Chaldeans, one to the Caucasian, &c. When he was asked if he could trace some of their families on earth, " Not able through the parents in spirit ; but I trace Mrs. K——'s family from her being present in form." Of this a very tangible example was shown. Much interesting matter

was given, mostly personal, not essential here. Those
persons traced I intimately knew on earth. I could but
notice the characteristics they showed to the people they
were said to have partaken of.

In taking leave of this subject, it is not inappropriate to
remark, after the clear and vivid manner in which it has
been presented, there may still remain questions of doubt,
and dislikes of its tenor and utility. But let it always
be remembered, that life after death in the individual is
the continued existence of memory; and your own individuality depends on your memory of life and all its
events : this you can not lay aside, and be yourself. I have
found, that, in spirit, memory is even more acute, active,
sharper even in *minutiæ*, than on earth. If this is so,
what must be the state of some spirits who find it impossible to evade the memory of themselves? It is a remorse
unbearable. To carry this with them continually is to
suffer everlasting hell-torments. Therefore forgetfulness
of personality is rest from this activity, and is the heaven
they seek, one that the soul craves to find, and the ultimate purifying of the same. The angelic spheres remote
from earth are of light, purity, and intelligence, and not
the conglomerated mass of all that is vile and hideous from
humanity without distinction. Put reason in the balance-
scale, and weigh it. Can Nature's law be evaded? Will
soul not aspire to its acme of attainments, rather than
retain the memory of some half-fledged intellect? It is its
own judge and purifier, and its judgments can not be re-
sisted. In this respect, it carries its own divine essence.
But these rehabiting souls do not take lower rank as punishment : contrariwise, they come higher, and in subsequent forms are the best and brightest minds, often the
most moral and brilliant intellects. That much has been
given contrary to the accepted tenets of the many teach

ings from others is true: for this very purpose, it is
intended to be the forerunner of breaking light.

> Learn, of the earth you are;
> To earth you will return,
> Unless you are adapted
> For the spheres divine.
>
> Life is but a scale,
> Ascending round by round:
> When one step is made complete,
> The future ones begin.
>
> Soul is but intelligence;
> In the least it's shown:
> When you see it thus expressed,
> Remember to be kind.
>
> For each may say
> With truth divine,
> "You are ahead this time;
> But I am of your kind."

PART II.

OCCULT FORCES IN MAN.

WEBSTER's definition of occult is, "Hidden from the eye or understanding; invisible; secret; unknown; undiscovered; undetected."

This I use as the true and appropriate term to convey the hidden forces in man, or the power of soul to manifest itself.

The subject is too deep and expansive to be contained within a volume, and it is not in the ability of one mind to fathom its depths. Our poor ability can only convey inklings, that others may take up the chain, add a link, or follow it out in some branch.

If one could read the universe, search into every identical soul, and read its manifestations, then might he know occultism; but we opine that no one mind, be it on earth or in spirit, is so endowed.

Occultism being the science of the soul's forces, it necessarily takes in all past time, and is no new-fangled conception relating only to the present manifestations and nature of being. In ages past, minds and intelligences have made the attempt to search into and probe these forces; but the ages, times, and conditions were not cal-

culated to convey a solution, give a satisfactory reply, or
impart a knowledge of a power they did not understand.
From time to time, individual minds have made some
attempt in the same direction, but with very little success.
At the present age and time, when scientists are explor-
ing earth and heaven for cause and effect, man and his
relation to the forces he gives out, they have given expression to various terms to convey an idea not well understood ; such as ''odyllic force,'' ''psychic force,'' '' spirit
force,'' ''nervous aura,'' ''magnetism,'' ''cerebration,''
etc. These form a multiplicity of scientific names for one
and the same thing, —occult force, or the soul manifesting
its conscious power. Let them go to the inner man, the
cause of being and its expression, and there search and
find a solution to what they never yet gave a satisfactory
explanation of, representing these powers to be elements,
substances, conditions, or some special peculiarity in the
atomic structure, etc., that acts without consciousness or
guidance. But, if they would look into the dynamical relation of soul to its organism, a true light would guide their
searching. If they would but learn the duality of being,
that it is matter moved by soul, the whole subject would
be clear to their comprehension. The human mind is so
constituted, that it soars beyond itself. This is the result
of a consciousness of the fact that there is something yet
to be reached, something to fill the void. In order to
know a power, its seat, location, and channels should be
understood ; for this is here shown the structure of the
brain, and the seat of power. The brain is an organ in
all animals that have senses. In the human its structure
is composed of cerebrum and cerebellum. The upper
and larger cerebrum is divided into two hemispheres : the
lower surface of this organ is again divided into three
lobes, — the anterior, the middle, and the posterior. The

cerebellum is about one-sixth the size of the cerebrum, and takes in the medulla oblongata, and most of the nerves centre here. The three lobes on the lower surface of the cerebrum rest, the anterior on the skull, the posterior on the cerebellum, forming one organ, which, with its ramifications and nerve-centre, is the seat of sensation.

In the middle lobe of the cerebrum, and resting on the cerebellum and the space between what would be immediately above the roof of the mouth and the very centre of the whole organ, is the seat and throne of the soul, the spirit-centre.

To physiologists, on analysis, this could not be detected ; for, while there is a vital spark, the interior of the brain is inaccessible : but to the spirit, the clear-seer, this may be apparent. But one external evidence exists that the whole brain is not the seat of life. It is well authenticated by medical practice, that many instances of injury to the outside of the brain exist. A bullet has passed through its surface, and skulls have been trepanned, without destroying life ; but, should a bullet be sent through its centre, it results in instant death. One other fact can be observed, — that its location is near the nerve-centre, the cerebellum, or external sensation. Indications seem to show that here is located a small, oscillating, insect-light, not precisely alike in all except in location. From this centre radiates a glow and luminosity throughout the whole, not always equal, but varying according to conditions. Here, then, are located the life-principle, the soul-forces in the sensorium, sending telegraphic currents through the nerves to every part of the form and its mental and physical functions. In fact, the spirit is the sensorium, the only seat.

It is well known, by analyzing the substance of the brain, that there is nothing within that indicates its peculiar sensitiveness or its intelligent nature more than there is in the blood. In every individual it has the same conformation, substance, and nerves ; though every person has a different mentality and expression of intellect, and the brain is said to be the organ of mentality.

If the brain of itself could think, being all of the same structure and substance, there would be a uniformity of mentality, as all the other organs act throughout all humanity alike. But this organ is evidently the seat of some special power. It is, in fact, the abiding-place of the soul, the battery operated by it; and, just as soon as the soul vacates, there is no power or force to move the machinery.

It has been said that from this central light was evolved a glow of luminosity. This can be seen by clairvoyants, and is thrown out sometimes in a halo around the head. One's own vision can often be inverted, and see this glow through the brain. The writer has done it many times in years past. Spirits have experimented, and shown her the location of this little thing of matter, light, and activity, — the spirit. It has a ceaseless action, electro-dynamic in its forces. This is no chimera or fanciful picture, but a condition of facts all may become cognizant of. The sensation being in the spirit, it is through the spirit every one of the senses are felt; the nerves and organs being leaders and instruments to connect our inner selves with the external world, acting as telegraph-wires ; and, when any one of these is cut, there is no connection made with the sensorium, and that part is lost. The brain-tissues are liable to disease, the same as any other part ; and when the brain is so diseased it is a bad instrument, similar to a battery out of order, and its action would be about as incorrect. As the spirit grows and develops with the form, it becomes the mental and physical stereotype of the same. As you find the individual, so is his spirit; no more nor less. I have never found this law to vary in the most familiar acquaintance with embodied and disembodied man. As spirit draws its conditions through the senses with the external life, the bad uses, habits, and vices belong to it as much as would exceptional virtues, subject to the law of change and progress.

It has been said by some, that the thoughts and acts of life are photographed on the brain, to be seen by those in spirit-life. This is not the action of the brain; but, as spirit fills and acts through it like electricity, all its thoughts and acts become mirrored there, and disembodied spirit draws them out. Spirit reaches spirit more directly than earthly man.

The soul of man being a principle that has already partaken of many of Nature's conditions, sensing its relation to all soul and its power, placed in the human brain to be clothed with intelligent spirit, it may exercise many forces, which the external world is rarely, if ever, willing to concede. This power exerts itself both in mundane and supermundane life. Conscious of this relation to spirit, it may externalize this, and bring the two in rapport, by sight, hearing, psychometry, and mesmerism. These are not medial powers or gifts, but the property of the soul that can convey them to the external senses. The two spheres are never wholly separated. Sleep is an unconscious state of the external senses. The spirit does not sleep wholly, but it rests; that is, it ceases from activity and motion, draws in its forces, and may adopt an independent action for a short time.

Dreams are the strongest evidence of a mind outside of the senses. Mesmerism, or animal magnetism, is supposed to be a peculiar and mysterious nature, by which a powerful influence may be exerted on one person by another. This is the exercise of a force in the organism superior to that in another. Each soul takes on some peculiar elements, and these are thrown out through the organism. If there is a consciousness of this strength, there may be exercised a will-power over another who is more passive, and make him subject to the will of the stronger. This force is much more exercised than humanity supposes. It is the attractive or repelling force any one may feel from another, and the soul's indicator of its sensitiveness to another's elements. Disembodied spirit exercises this power to a great extent; for it is a universal law, that soul is recognized by its elements.

Clairvoyance, or clear-sightedness, is a power in persons of discerning things not present to the senses. It has been shown that the brain is only an instrument which through nerves connects with the external, and is not the power. The power is the spirit: take away the instrument, and the power that exercised it can just as well do the same in the interior light. The spirit is then able to see independently things of the interior life; and, as things of the spirit are imparted, they are conveyed to the external consciousness. The elements or conditions of clear-seeing are in the conditions of the individual, and are not common to all.

The same of clairaudience. All the same laws operate and apply to this power as to clairvoyance. The writer possesses this power to an exalted extent, and can speak from knowledge and experience of its capabilities, the proof of which is in the lessons conveyed in these pages. It is a power extending in all directions, mundane and supermundane; is not restricted by space; and proves that the spirit may become so acute as to hear from the most distant spheres while yet inhabiting the earthly form. At the same time, the mind may give out a force of thought that will reach higher spheres, and be responded to. I am not dependent on the supernal world for a demonstrated knowledge of this fact of clairaudience, and that, while it places one in communication with denizens of distant spheres, it includes the sphere on earth as well. Having friends, connections, and family thousands of miles distant from me, I have heard them in converse as distinctly as though present. At one time I sat an hour listening to an interview between two of my family a thousand miles from me, every word of which was afterwards found to be correct. I have had very many proofs that those on earth at a distance from each other can send out their thoughts, and receive responses, as promptly and correctly as though they sat side by side.

There is another force, or power, that is yet dormant in its exercise, and rarely thought of by humanity. This is mental telegraphy, one of the most agreeable of mental powers. It consists in being able to send and receive a message from living and distant friends, as well as those who have removed from earthly action. I have exercised this to an extent that would require pages and pages to fully record. I have tested its reality with entire strangers whose names I only knew; and rarely found that they would not respond, when the time was auspiciously chosen. Members of my family have been as communicative as though in my presence. I have even trained them to be familiar with the mode of communication, so that they would readily respond when a call was made. Here, for the benefit of all others, is given the manner of procedure. It is a well-established fact, that the mind will not have two thoughts at the same instant of time. Therefore, if a person's attention is engaged when they are called with things of the external life, there will be more or less diversion or confusion. This is apt to be the case during their wakeful hours; and for this reason the hour of slumber is the best to choose, the mind being then less likely to be engaged with external matters. Fix your mind earnestly on the object desired; then mentally call the name, make some pleasant remark, and ask your question. If the person addressed is disengaged, he will respond; and, if you are in a good clairaudient state, you will hear the reply.

I once called to a compositor engaged at his stand, not thinking of his night occupation. He gave some reply; when he said, " I wish you would let me alone : I cannot set my matter, and get through in time; and I'm tired now." I have made many tests in this line, and have learned by them that there should be a concentration of thought in the minds of both persons. Disembodied spirits are accessible by the same procedure.

If spirit in form can dispatch thoughts or ideas unconscious to its external senses to another fully conscious of receiving them, it is only from the fact that the last is more externalized in spirit than the first; and the first might be equally so, if educated to the same extent.

This is the exhibit of the mental telegraph that will be the universal means of correspondence when future ages shall have developed the powers of spirit in man.

Such is a brief synopsis of the source of the occult forces in man, practical and accessible to all who would understand their being, and learn that the powers within them are beyond what the external senses can at present realize.

The subject is continued, extended, and illustrated through the remainder of this volume, the aim of which is to elucidate the nature of man's inner life, and its exercise, and relation to others, and to show, that, embodied or disembodied, each individual's forces are his

own, and not to be blended with or lost in those of
another.

DUALITY.

Duality is the state of being double, — that is, to maintain a personality in two places at the same time, — and is
the most interesting phenomenon of our being. If there is
any thing that would satisfy a mind of life outside of the
earthly form, or of the action of mind without matter, it
is this ; because, if there is a second principle that can
act temporarily, independent of the material senses, it will
be evident that it can be extended indefinitely, and indicates that there is something intelligent existing independent of the physical.

As this phase of our being is universal, as it is the
corner-stone of our nature, as it shows plainly the relation of spirit and matter, it is most important for us to
know ; and therefore the space here allotted to its exhibit
will not be considered wasted. I have shown in " Occult
Forces in Man " that the spirit is a small thing of matter,
light, and activity, having its place in the centre of the
brain. That it can act independent of the brain, nerves,
and even of the whole physical, is the subject of this
chapter. The spirit is electro-dynamic, which constitutes
its power of force and motion. When so inclined, it can
withdraw from the brain like a spark of light, and be all
of self without it. In doing this, while there is life in
the body, there is always a current connecting the two.
This current looks like a streak, or band, and not unlike a
comet's tail, connecting the two ; and through this current
there is an unbroken sensation with the form. It is only
at death this current can be broken. It can be jarred, or
it may vibrate. It will be seen that through this current
of connection the spirit may be affected by the conditions

of the physical or its disturbing causes. In this way it may travel any distance, and manifest to a person who can be made sensible of its presence.

The most tangible manner to illustrate this action, and show its phases, will be to give an account of manifestations made to the writer. By this means the subject can be practically understood. Facts are better than theories, and my purpose is to substantiate statements by proof. As these experiences have been quite unusual and varied, they are most likely to interest, and show duality in its strongest light.

In the year 1875 I resided a thousand miles from an intimate friend, a lady of threescore and ten, a person of much experience, and a well-marked character of positive will. One morning, after some representations in regard to her had been made by a spirit, I requested another spirit to find out the truth of the statements ; when, in a short time, she very unexpectedly made her personal presence known, so real that it staggered me. The hour was about the time she would be rising.

This was my first introduction to this kind of manifestation, and I very naturally concluded she was in spirit-life. She was frantic with excitement, stating she must be dead, and that she was murdered, and showing a high state of feeling at what had befallen her. She gave true and exact relations of her character and belongings, referring to things between us, so that I could not make a mistake in regard to her identity. Suddenly she left, then returned in a few minutes, — if any thing, more perturbed than at first. In this way she made three trips in one hour, each time giving some agitated conjectural account of what must have caused her exit from the body, and her troubles about what would be done with it. In asking how she came to call on me, she said a lady brought her. Her whole demeanor was excited and irregular; yet it was full of proofs of her identity.

I heard nothing more from her for two months; when one day she made her presence known very tangibly, and as natural as it was possible for her to be. She described minutely the details of events that transpired after I left her, and in which I was one of the parties most concerned, showing her feelings in regard to them with remarkable perspicuity. She travelled round my room, took observations, and was generally busy for one hour. I was fully under the conviction she was in spirit-life: for this reason I questioned her considerably on her condition, and how she was suited. I noticed she would have nothing to say of spirit-things, or of her being there. When questioned on the subject, her replies were, "Time's time; let it rest; all time is my time; I shall move slow and sure:" then again revert to her own feelings, and repeat, "Time's time; all time is time; I'm not in haste." After this second very demonstrative visit, I wrote to a mutual friend to inform me in regard to her. In due time a reply came, stating that she was not dead, but in her usual condition. This disturbed my ideas of spirit-things. I felt myself deceived and imposed on by something that must be explained. I reasoned in this wise: "If some false spirit can so perfectly assume and act the individuality of another person, then it's not safe to have them near: I'll clean them out." Time brought its own revealments, as I have ever found it will. Only a short time elapsed when she called on me again, this time in the night. She introduced herself by repeating, "Time's time, and time's again: all time I have." After a few remarks, I questioned her about the other visits. She said, "I sat me down by my stand, and thought to send out an impression to you; when I went to sleep immediately, and made a visit instead.'' After this she visited me a couple of times. The last time she said, "Mrs. K——, why don't you return my calls? You have not called on me yet. I shall stay away if you don't.''

Thus this old soul showed all its intuitive knowledge of its relation to time, and practices the same in external life ; for it is her peculiarity not to be hasty, but precise : at the same time, she is a remarkable woman generally.

In the interim another was visiting me, an old friend, a gentleman of eighty-six years. All his calls were in the daytime and sunlight. He entered the open door, called me by name, and talked in the most familiar manner ; handled things I showed him ; told me of returning to the Eastern States ; and every thing we could think of we talked about. I questioned him about his family in spirit-life, and of his own condition. His replies were evasive, — that he could not or had not seen them, was solitary, and knew nothing of spirit. In a week or two he called again, sat on the lounge, and chatted for a time ; when I made a remark that caused him to leave like a flash. After a couple of weeks he called again, and stood beside me in nubilous form with a large stick. I remarked about his large cane ; when he raised it, and said, " I like my old hickory stick best : it has strength and support.'' A few moments after he left, I immediately wrote to those that knew him, and informed them he was in spirit-life. In due time a reply came that he was not ; that they were in company with him at such a date, and he had but recently returned to the Eastern States. Two years later, at this writing, he is living and well. The reply was astonishing to me ; for he had been more tangible than the woman, and I was not then aware I was receiving visits from the spirits of those living on earth, while I knew I could not mistake the characters of those I so well knew.

Another friend called once, at night, to answer my letter in person. She approached by calling my name, and said, "I am not dead, but come to let you know I am so sick, and my cares and vexations so trouble me, I can't answer your letter." She went on to converse on every familiar subject; told me of her condition, the place she had removed from, of her family affairs; said she could not live long; that when she was in spirit-life she would inform me. Her visit must have been one hour.

Others made one visit each, whom I afterwards found were not dead. The most marvelous of these visitants was one of my own family, and shows one of the most striking proofs of this phase of the mind's action. One night a young man approached, calling, "Mother, mother! don't be alarmed, and think I'm lost or gone. I have only called to see you, and let you know of myself." After which he entered into a familiar recital of what concerned him; when he bade me good-night, and left. A week or two after he made me another call, about in the same manner, but of shorter duration. Some weeks later he made a third trip, while there were present several disembodied spirits. He approached, calling, "Mother, mother!" when, saying a few words quietly, he grasped me with a horrified feeling of fright, making every nerve in me quake; then he took on a raving state of delirium, thrilling my whole system with his sensations of fright. He raved about those he had an interest in, saying some misfortune had befallen them; and kept calling on me with frantic delirium to aid him in his troubles. All I could say would not pacify nor soothe his wild distress. I expostulated, and begged to know why he should be so unreasonable, and told him he had better leave; when he instantly did so. I requested an old spirit present (Cenis) to follow him up, and see what the trouble was.

When he had returned to his form, and the spirit sooth-
ingly talked to him, calling him by his name, he said,
" Mother's spirits ! She may keep her spirits. They frightened me to death. I don't want them, and I sha'n't go
where she is with her spirits." Then he related how he
had visited the ocean, after the loss of the steamship
" Pacific," to find some of the drowning people he thought
he would rescue ; when some of their spirits attacked him
for his life, and threatened they'd drown him ; and he
had such a tussle with them, and became so frightened,
that the next day he was quite sick. We expostulated
with him not to try such trips ; that I did not consider it
right, and an injury to young people ; further, I wanted
no more such visits. This last trip was but two weeks
after the going-down of that steamer with her freight
of human lives, that gave such a sensation of horror to
the community.

I asked for an explanation why he should have acted
so frantic, and was told that it probably was as he represented ; that he might have had some encounter, became
frightened, and the elements did not suit him. At this
time the cause of all this trouble was, that a spirit was
present whose elements were in antagonism and repellent
to him. Although he did not see or know who were present,
nor did they approach him, yet he sensed the element so
acute, it immediately filled him with horror. As soon as
he was at home in his form, he could be as social as possible. He was not at all shy of spirits that were congenial ;
for one of his own age, who had been an associate, con-
versed nightly with him, and even posted him on things
transpiring that concerned him. This young man was by
no means a frail, delicate sensitive, but of remarkable
physical and mental vigor, executive power, and magnetic
forces.

These rambling people are very shy of all disembodied spirits, and do not remain long with them. They are capable of being greatly affected by them if they think themselves in danger. The body is their castle, and they do not like to have this castle disturbed. Young people are more sensitive, as in the case of the young man finding himself in the presence of repellent elements after his late encounter. His first impulse was to cling to me, and call piteously for my assistance to avert some anticipated danger. So long as there is connection with the body through its current, they are in sympathy with its condition. Thus a spirit on its excursions will be more or less disturbed by those conditions ; as in the case of the first visit from the woman. It was near her time of rising when a spirit disturbed her. Being advanced in years, and not in good health, she naturally anticipated her death ; and, under the disturbing condition she was in, an uneasy, frantic state exhibited itself. This leads to the query, Is there delirium in spirit-life ? Most certainly there is in the first sphere of action. I have often seen it in those who can not place themselves in spirit, yet are not of earth. They seem to be without location ; sometimes very frantic.

In connection with this subject the writer is reluctantly necessitated to give her own individual experiences, conscious to the external senses ; trusting the reader will be just, and not consider them approaching the incredulous, and hoping they may prove interesting and instructive to all who would know how they are organized, and by what power they act.

In the summer of 1875, I had been for several months continually in the company of spirits. For several days they had been using a force something like magnetism on me, showing cosmos through my brain. This is a process the reader would not credit if told : so I leave it for

the future life to reveal to them. Even for myself, I do
not understand the law that governs it: I only know of
its effects. It was a revolving of luminosity, showing a
panorama of past conditions, and the chain of incidents
that follow one, and its relation to all things. Finally
they trenched on what I considered forbidden ground. I
did not like it: besides, my brain had become so electric,
I could see the whole process myself. I felt it was of
little use to complain : so I hastily arose and went to bed,
and slept all night. Early next morning, when I awoke, all
my company of the evening before were present. Immè-
diately an intelligence passed from the inner to the outer,
and began to talk rapidly to them, without any action of
the brain or physical forces whatever. Up to this time,
in my converse with these visitors, I had talked through
the mind by thoughts ; but this was totally different. It
was outside of any action of the brain, like a second self,
with more force and strength ; and it would act independent of the organism. It told them to stand back, not to
approach ; and it would show them it was able to control
itself, and did not intend to put up with imposition, and
what a fine class they were of inferiors. After a running
talk, one of those present, who had been a companion in
life, was taken for the purpose of analyzing his career and
the conditions that had existed between us. This was
done in a lecture of one hour, and in rapid, fluent, well-
chosen language. I was myself much surprised at the
memory, and the manner of using it with such facility.

The whole class was awe-struck, ashamed for results,
and became restless under fire and shot; and the matter became so unpleasant to them, that the intelligence
told them the remainder would be deferred until the next
morning, but she should ⁻be mistress of itself, and not
subject to their conditions. At this I hastily jumped out

of bed. The three following mornings, as soon as I awoke, the subject was resumed under the same conditions, style, and characteristics, criticising the relations and conditions that had existed all round. It will be observed, this took place immediately after a night's refreshing sleep ; no dreams nor disturbing conditions ; the physical and mental fresh and rested, and the first wakeful moments improved. There is no attributing the facts to abnormal conditions, visions, trances, or outside influences of spirit. The whole external senses were fully conscious, but passive.

This manifestation so startled one of my more progressed and longer-in-spirit-life friends, that she made application to others still more progressed to visit and analyze the spirit. This brought in several more advanced to the analysis. My brain had become so electric, I sensed every move or thought one of them made. No approach could be made in my atmosphere without my knowing it : so no concealment was attempted. (The whole procedure I could not convey, and it would be irrelevant to the subject.) An unusual conversation ensued to and fro between the spirit in earth-form and a lady in spirit-life, who said she had come to take such a witch of a spirit out of its hiding-place, to clip its wings, or make it fly. By cajolery, playfulness, and congeniality, the spirit was induced to exit to the external. I saw it start, fly, and circle round before me like an electric insect, all the while talking as usual, and return as it started ; while the others said, " There, Mrs. K——, is your own spirit."

From this moment I was a dual person : the spirit would talk to the external consciousness, answer questions, correct and reprimand what did not suit, and I could hear its ideas expressed in the brain. The statements were, it never had gone on trips or excursions from the body to any distance; never was conscious of doing such a thing up to that time; that it was satisfied with the organism, and wished to remain by it, and would not yield control to another; was familiar with the ideas and whisperings of spirits and those in close rapport. There were no further manifestations in this respect for six months. Rest had been taken from spirit-things in general, and business attended to. After this complete rest, a new phase of things came about. The spirits started fresh, and some of the incidents heretofore related in these pages took place.

The guide here mentioned was a developing guide, and had been two thousand years in spirit-life.[1]

From two or three gathered to confer and be entertained, others would come, until a vast concourse of spirits would be present, coming and going. One subject after another was discussed; when Cenis entered to entertain them in a new light by exhibiting me in two forms at the same time, — one of flesh and one of spirit, the intelligence blended in the two. The manner of proceeding was in this way: A circle was formed of congenial and harmonious friends to take up their position close to the body and round the head. This band, as I shall call them, that closely surrounded my person, were individuals that had been, at various times in my life, friends when I most needed them. Outside of these, round the room, were a larger number in a circle, perhaps twenty. Surrounding

---

[1] It is objected by many persons, that the Indian has too great prominence in the manifestations of Spiritualism. I hope not to offend the taste if I inform the reader that this Cenis was an American Indian, belonging to the central and northern territory in the Black-hill country, and of the same race as the Sioux. He has given liberal accounts of what the country was like at one time in its population, and the interest taken by the spheres in its discovery and settlement by the whites. He has proved a friend and guide indeed to me, and I trust will guide me still farther on, even on the shores beyond; while this is the only poor tribute I can give of him and his services and attention to me.

this circle were still a greater number, numbering two or three hundred. These were all disembodied spirits gathered to witness what was taking place in my humble abode. The time chosen for this manifestation was always morning and evening, while I was reclining in a chair, or in bed before rising. When things were in condition, the spirit would leave the form, draw around itself elements of matter, take Cenis by the hand, and walk round among those present; talking to each one, shaking hands, sitting beside them, analyzing, and giving each one his or her allotted place; talking of old and familiar memories, and enjoying in general social converse. While this was performing with the spirit-part, the body and senses were perfectly normal, fully realizing the whole. At the same time, I knew what was transpiring in the external just as well; and the spirit would respond to every move or impression made on the brain, even by vibration. But I could not hold a thought only as the spirit could convey it. Every idea was in consonance with its movements. There did not exist two thoughts, or double ideas: it was simply two persons with one intelligence. This exercise would last for hours, — holding the most familiar intercourse, spirit to spirit, with old friends, and strangers as well; and the same was repeated day after day.

The spirit-form was not so large by a third or fourth as my full stature; so it was small: but the intellect seemed to be more sharp and active, by no means weak. I felt it was the oddest performance; and this narration of it will hardly convey any true idea of its reality. The moment the body would rise up from reclining, the spirit would re-enter, and the whole form would shiver and quake with intense cold as in an ague-fit, chattering, and throwing out the tongue exceedingly. It was a peculiar sensation, different from any thing I ever felt before. The force of this also depended on the length of time the spirit was out : this was sometimes hours, morning and evening.

After this had continued some days, and familiarity and confidence gained, Cenis gave the hand to another to lead a lady who had but recently entered spirit-life, and well known on earth and in spirit as a public medium. By this hand this being of earth and spirit was led round among this assembly of disembodied people in the room ; while they would only shake hands with 'it, and ask the questions of the lady-spirit. Drawing to the final, Cenis took the being under his wing, and away he went into space. He presented it to an assembly of American statesmen ; when they said, " We salute you as an American lady ; " then asked Cenis if he was not going too far. This required but a few moments. The next day the third going into space was tried.

The last time it passed still farther. For an instant it seemed as though connection was lost or drawn off, and I lost consciousness like a sudden going-out of a candle. My encircling band did not like this, and thought Cenis had done too much. However, this was my last fly into space, and the close of these exercises.

It might be thought by most persons that these things would be unpleasant. Not so ; but, on the contrary, quite enjoyable. The only unpleasant thing was the excessive cold and shivering that supervened. The cause of this shiver was, that, the spirit had so long been in the element of disembodied spirit, the return gave a change to the currents. Theirs was brought in ; while the magnetic forces had been drawn from the body, and the counter-currents were chilling.

In this manifestation was not only duality, but three principles shown, — the external form, the spirit-form, and the intelligence that exercised both at the same time ; a trinity, absolutely conscious to one person, — body, soul, and spirit. Such, then, is the absolute make-up of our natures while sojourners in the external world of matter. But really duality is the mind acting in some place outside of the brain, while the form is not used; and this may be done without material or spirit-form, as in the instance of all my visitors of earth living at a distance from me. I have given much space to the introduction of proof on this subject, deeming it the solid foundation of past, present, and future being. If any one can convey a higher proof of duality, it is due to humanity to know of it. It is unquestionable evidence of intelligence outside of form, and independent of matter, that soul is the principle of intelligence.

Because a person's spirit rambles off to distant scenes while in sleep, it does not follow that it is any the better acquainted with spirit-things. It may not be willing to come in contact with them in one condition more than in another. It is impossible for one to go into distant spheres, and it is impracticable while the conditions of earth are carried with them. If the cord becomes too attenuated, it will break; and the spirit could not retake the form, neither could it be connected with body from a distant sphere. Besides, there is a law that repels such things, and says,

> "Child of earth thou art, and earthly things thou mayst explore;
> But things beyond this earth in time will be thy store."

I am aware that some entertain the idea, that, in sleep, they explore and bask in the domains of superior spheres, delighting, perhaps, in trips to distant planets. Not so: no spirit can surpass itself. The spirit-sight may be extended, and take in visions of the beyond. Spirits may be near to psychologically present pictures, and the memory of the individual thus seeing may retain them in waking hours; but do not flatter yourself you have gone beyond your sphere. Nature does not allow a violation of her laws; nor will one go in the body, nor out of it, beyond its sphere, until it has made progress to that plane. Therefore these rambling people visit scenes of earth and those they are familiar with, and not beyond. Somnambulism — walking, talking in sleep when the senses are closed to the external — is an illustration of this nature. The spirit moves the form without the action of its senses, evidence of which is often witnessed. Some adopt the idea that a foreign spirit takes possession of and moves the body round. This is not so. It is the restless element within themselves. The proof of this is in the fact that they almost invariably resort to objects and places familiar to them in their wakeful hours. The inimitable Shakspeare has ably shown its action in his Lady Macbeth, whose restless spirit is so exercised to wash itself from blood. No one need expect to typify it better.

CLAIRVOYANCE AND PSYCHOLOGY.

In "Occult Forces in Man," it is said clairvoyance is not medial, but the action of one's own powers. This does not imply, nor is it intended to mean, that every thing seen by a clairvoyant is a genuine spirit-object or of spirit-life. There are different phases and forms of this power. Probably not more than one-tenth are actual visions of true spirit-conditions, or realities of those spheres. They are psychological effects produced by spirits, or the medium's surroundings, for some purpose known to themselves. It is the mesmeric effect the operator conveys to his subject. The seer is operated on in the same way. One may be conveyed for hours through a panoramic vision of all the Elysian fields of spheres beyond, or, reversely, the regions of inferno, and be under psychological control.

Spirit-guides love to practice those things to entertain their mediums. When it is known that every event of one's life is photographed on the brain, it will be seen how readily a spirit may select from them, and present it to their medium.

Pictures, emblems, or symbols, presented of persons or things, are thus a form of entertainment. As the spirit sees them, it may be called psychological clairvoyance.

But genuine seership is to know that it is an intelligence that is expressing itself, and shows what it is. If it can not give something besides the generalities that a guide can convey, it is to be distrusted.

The true seership is peculiar, and not conveyed by another. It is a quick perception of interior things. It is an opening-out, and not a drawing-in. Seeing of supernal things, or a quick perception of the nature of things, is of the soul, and inspirationally given to the consciousness ; and some law controls it not easily explained.

As an illustration, however, of how this power may be exercised, and the many phases it takes, I will give a few examples. Some years since, after going to bed and becoming easy and rested, not asleep, I would see small figures, half-forms, feet, hands, faces like those of children grinning at me, but nothing regular. They would pass me like groups, and perhaps return. This was repeated night after night. In regard to this peculiar exhibit, I inquired at the time what it meant.

Answer. — The sensorium having taken on impressions of external things, when the eyes are closed the impression is there, and it may be seen in an inverted condition. Then there is another phase : the seer may not be able to take in all the appearances or form of a spirit trying to show itself, or in their presence ; and it appears misshapen. Perhaps this appearance is caused by the spirit not being able to convey a well-defined appearance, and consequently gives but a part. It often happens that the seer is not strong in giving elements for spirits to show by. It must be remembered that spirits draw from the person they are seen by; and they may not be strong enough to gather these elements. They are intelligences of their sphere, nevertheless.

Question. — Is there such a thing as half-souls, or elements without souls manifesting intelligence?

Answer. — Where there is intelligence, there must be soul. It is impossible to be otherwise.

Question. — Does ethereal matter take shape, act, and influence, or manifest intelligently to man?

Answer. — Not in any way, shape, or manner. Matter can not act intelligently if there is not intelligence or soul with it. Intelligence may act in a very imperfect, rude, or crude way; yet it is there.

Where there is a manifestation of distinguishing power, there is soul, though it may be affected by elemental conditions, — the same as a child might scream, and not tell by language why it did so. If matter could act in such a way, what would be the results? There would be no difference between them, and the soul of man would be without preference or distinction.

That spirits give any variety of pictures and symbols is true, from the most lofty down to the most ridiculous, as it suits them, or those they wish to entertain. Unfortunately, these are often taken for substantial realities of spirit-life. For instance, if a spirit shows you some emblem he fancies, it is no proof it is real. The next time, or some time in the future, you may find out it had no reality. In the year 1875 a near friend in spirit-life was anxious I should see him, and said he would make me do so. After a while a lovely child was looking right in my face, with its

big blue eyes, flaxen curls, white dress, and blue ribbons.
I exclaimed, "What a lovely child!" when he said,
"That's my child." No reference was made to it again:
but, months after, something was said to his sister, also in
spirit, about his child; when it was shown there was no
such child in spirit. It was his memory of a child twenty
years past, not dead, but now a young man. I could see
the picture he thought of, but not him. Some months
later, a well-known American divine who had gone to
Italy for his health, and there died, being with a number
of others present and experimenting, I saw very clearly a
lovely ring — to me a perfect gem — of emerald green,
with a white crescent upon it, and white star below the
crescent. The mounting and ring were of fine copper wire
like a thread. It was so peculiar in this respect, I could
but notice it. Immediately I exclaimed, "What a lovely
gem!" when he replied, "You see it well: but it is not a
natural gem; it is manufactured." Then others wanted
to see it; and he gave its history. It was a mosaic ring,
made at a place he visited in Italy to see the mosaic
works. This one thing took his fancy: so he bought and
wore it, and thus had shown it to me to test the strength
of vision, at the same time to exhibit to me a curiosity.
Afterwards came statues and other works of art. Others
then tried what they could bring out; and soon a small
fancy dog, white, with black spots, stood before me. I
did not hear him growl nor bark. It was done for effect,
to test my vision. Once there appeared, standing beside
me, a woman in walking attire of the old style, with one
of those enormous bonnets, big flowers, shawl, and dress
so gay, all *à la Dolly Varden*. I could but notice it, and
remarked, "What a gaudy thing!" when I was told,
"It's only an image."

These examples show how real a lifeless representation

may appear to a seer, and that a semblance may be mistaken for a reality; as I took the child to be in the first instance, until I was better informed, and they showed what imagery was. This, perhaps, is more phenomenal than clear or independent seeing; for it is the process of spirits calling up the memory of things past in such a way that they are transmitted to the seer in pictures. The test of true seership is the ability not to mistake these for genuine spirit-realities. The intelligence should indicate the nature of the thing, and that it may be simulated by a guide. Once I had a guide who had been a nun in a convent, and a teacher among children. One evening a poor child was introduced. A chatty little talk commenced of its poor conditions and relations in life, and it adopted me for its instructor. These visits were kept up for a week. Other children came in the mean time, and told their story of affluence and fine relations. Thus it passed back and forth, — first one class, then another. By and by I mistrusted something wrong, and called for an explanation.

Then I was informed it was simply a representation designed to show what the result of advantages and education would be in forming the mind and intellect. Thus what are looked upon as realities may be otherwise, even when the medium does not suspect it.

A spirit that was much interested in me suddenly appeared before me very plain, — color of dress and style as though material. Over her shoulder was seen the face of a young man for an instant. Shortly a young sailor-boy stood not far from me. The woman talked freely of family-affairs, and then said the likeness she showed me was that of her son when she last saw him, twenty-one years of age; and the sailor-boy was as she thought of him, intending to put him to sea. Thus this woman showed one person in two ways at different ages ; and I should have thought there were three spirits, if the explanation had not been given. I know she was truthful; for that son has been in spirit-life sixteen years, and was the companion of the writer : and on this occasion she pictured before my vision her memory of forty-one years or more.

Psychological effects can be carried to very great lengths, perhaps more than any other manifestation. Poor spirits resort to this on many occasions.

Although psychology is the doctrine of man's soul and spiritual nature, in my humble opinion it is the substratum of all physical manifestation, — embodied and disembodied minds ; and I do not consider it to be exercised always by the best intelligence. As disembodied mind comes in contact with elements, conditions, of other minds in external life, such are taken on, borrowed for the occasion ; and a manifestation may follow totally at variance with the true condition of that spirit. Thus a spirit may show itself in more ways than one ; increase its true stature to outward appearance, or lessen it as well.

Life in the external is but the selfsame law of manifesting. " Show me your company, and I'll tell you what you are." Therefore a trickster or juggler may have just such spirits as is wanted to aid him, and furnish the desired elements. Neither is any superior intelligence required in any psychological control. I will give an example of my experience to show how perfect this may be, and yet how deceptively untrue.

In the early part of 1875, a spirit and near connection was visiting me ; when one night she gave what purported to be a representation of a scene in a family on the Atlantic shores, three thousand miles distant. She began by the reception and reading of a letter from herself to them, and carried it into a high dramatic representation, and change of scenes and acts. She chose one child as clair-voyant medium — herself being the ghost to her medium — to operate on the rest of the family. The whole mani-festation was so realistic and highly dramatic, that I be-came convulsed with laughter. This she kept up all night (six hours), while I laughed most of the time, and thought it a genuine transaction that I was enjoying; when, at dawn of day, it ceased ; and suddenly a flash and concussion I felt to leave me, and I found it was only control. I had been six hours under psychological influence, in a conscious state, realizing the highest form of dramatic acting I ever witnessed. Nothing was said of it until months after, when — the same spirit being present, as also the one who had shown me the ring — I related to the latter her dramatic performance and talent. He asked her if she had ever been on the stage, and how she ope-rated her characters. Her reply was, " I used my fingers." This person had been in spirit-life at this time but two years and a half, and knew little of spirit-things. All her feelings were with her family on earth. Thus one that had no sympathy with spirit-life as yet had her mind so intently occupied with those she had left on earth, that she could personify all their peculiarities in a vividly active manner.

I might fill a volume showing from facts how disem-bodied spirits will take characters not particularly belong-ing to them, if they wish to do so, or have an object to accomplish. But this example sufficiently illustrates the fact.

Most of the extended visions said to be of spiritual life and spheres, in trance or out of trance, are only visions, — psychological effects produced by disembodied men, — and are no criterion for general things and conditions of the spheres beyond.

INSPIRATION AND PROPHECY.

Inspiration is the infusion of ideas or communications from superior powers, by some supposed to be a supernatural influence of the Spirit of God, or some other superior being, on the human mind.

Inspiration is the common property of every individual soul, not in the same direction, or to the same extent; but it is the power of the soul to draw in from universal intelligence what its necessities require. Every soul is sensitive to some extent to the forces operating in space, and to that extent will be affected by them. Each and every individual is conditioned to receive a proportional influx of superior ideas to execute a desired object. To say that it comes from some special superior being does not convey a correct idea of the truth. It is an all-pervading knowledge which fills space; and soul responds to soul in its desire for higher and greater force. There is an exchange of currents between the mundane and supermundane worlds of intelligence. Each gives an exchange with the other. If this was not so, there would be little intellectual progress made.

The advantages of the superior state gives a larger field of perception.

Inspiration has two distinct phases. It may be a disembodied spirit infusing its ideas into another, and so expressing them; or it may be independent, and drawn from the fountain-source. Such a person is gifted with a soul that can imbibe from a source that disembodied spirits are not superior to.

Inspiration is purely a law of the soul; and, when all its operating forces are understood, the full source of inspiration will be known.

Prophecy comes under the same heading, the explana-

tions thereof being nearly the same. Events forecast
their shadows. The condition of things may indicate the
results. Spirits see clearly through these conditions, and
therefore may convey it to another.

Independent prophecy is the same as inspiration.

Independent qualities of spirit belong as much to embodied as to disembodied mind.

SENSITIVES.

Sensitives are those that have quick and acute sensibilities, either to interior or exterior objects.

An idea has found extensive credence that all sensitives
are medial, or that all mediums are sensitive. This is
both truth and error, and leads to the query, What is a
medium? It is one who holds a middle place, — an instrument in the control of another.

There are so many phases of mediumship, that it would
be one of the most difficult of tasks to enumerate and
describe them all. But a person who exercises his own
gift can not properly be called a medium; and the terms
"sensitive" and "medium" are very often misapplied.
A sensitive is one whose spirit is acute to the elements
that approach him either interiorly or exteriorly; and his
sense may be so fine as to repel any outside control of
his organism, and be able to say, "I am monarch here,
and yield not my domain to another." Such are not
uncommon, and are of the finest minds. I have seen a
person so sensitive one could not touch him, and so full
of magnetism it could be seen, and as positive as one
could be, in whom there never was any phase of mediumship shown. It is the greatest mistake to suppose that
a medium must be of superior, fine sensibilities, mentally
or physically. Sometimes it is quite the other way, and
one who is a medium may be of the most inferior nature.

Thus there are sensitives without mediumship, and mediums without sensitiveness. This truth can be best illustrated by examples.

In California I knew a woman, of noticeable commanding physique and remarkable strong forces, who had no sensitiveness of spirit, or fineness of nature, whatever; not possessing even the common feelings of humanity; immoral in character, and of little virtue, — a person who never was in an assembly of spiritualists in her life; who disliked and would not hear any remarks on the subject, unless to treat them with gross derision; yet she was one of the most powerful of rapping mediums. Raps would be heard round the table at meal-times, — on the doors, chairs, floor, any place where wood was convenient, — while she was pursuing her work : for she never would sit for these manifestations, nor ask questions; but others present would ask mentally, and intelligent replies would be given. In this instance it was not sensitiveness, but her strong elements that were used.

Another I saw, who was considerably like the person just described, who had no mind but for dress and display; yet her mediumship has not been surpassed for powerful raps. If asked to rap with force, the response would give concussions sounding like that of a strong hand pounding down the door. Yet she was any thing but sensitive to fine feelings. I have known a man who had some of the best phases of test-mediumship, — raps, tips, pellets, and writing; and yet he was one of the most dissipated, immoral natures that ever society was afflicted with, and practiced every species of imposition in his dealings with his fellows. Thus it is seen that a fine sensitiveness does not always accompany good mediumship.

Physical mediums are those who are so constituted that

the elements in their organism can be drawn off to be used by the invisibles for the phase of mediumship they possess. It is this power they hold that is utilized and sought for, and not an inclination or nature for superior things. They are instruments adapted for a purpose, without regard to mental, moral, intellectual, or spiritual nature or qualities.

OBSESSION.

Obsession, although not specially one of the occult powers in man, bears relation to disembodied spirits. Obsession or possession, or the second spirit in the one form, is not uncommon, but only temporary. It is a disembodied spirit that connects itself with some person it fancies, or wishes to use, or to carry out some earthly purpose. Obsessing spirits are rarely advanced souls. It is a form employed at times to disinthrall from earthly conditions; for some spirits cannot advance out of, or throw off, earthly conditions, until they have done it through some living form. It is the most common mode of physical manifestation. A spirit that has possession will or can do almost any thing it will, if the spirit of the person so controlled gives way, or acts in concert with it. Such may stop a function of the body. I have known one to stop the action of deglutition, and throw a thing from the stomach; to change, lift, and carry at will, and exercise every power of the human form when conditions were favorable. Nearly all physical manifestations of mediums are of possession. The force is from within, outward. One spirit has possession, while a band may operate on the outside. A spirit rarely possesses a person without the consent of that person's spirit. It is either passively yielded, or the two may act together to produce an effect. Muscular writing without the will is the control of this outside power.

Trance is the passive yielding to another, or sometimes the giving up the whole form and action of the brain to another. A person's own spirit may entirely yield to another.

UNCONSCIOUSNESS, DELIRIUM, INSANITY.

As has been frequently stated in these pages, the state of the mind shows the condition of the spirit. It will be asked, " What of unconsciousness, delirium, dementa, or insanity, which are mental conditions?" A general reply would be, " The spirit is affected."

Unconsciousness is a true insensibility, — loss of the power to take in mental or physical conditions. That the spirit while associated with form and earthly conditions is affected by the same, is evident. That it is so, I know from the many showings I have had from disembodied mind.

There are very many causes producing unconsciousness. Any thing that produces stupor of the intellect must affect it, — drugs, narcotics, anæsthesias. The physical ailments will, and are very apt to, hasten the dissolution of the body.

That unconsciousness exists in another state is also true ; but of this it is not here necessary to speak.

Delirium — a wild, irregular, disconnected, untruthful state of the mind — is a temporarily disturbed state of the spirit, either in or out of the form, and results from physical, mental, or elemental conditions, or perhaps from all combined.

That the spirit may be affected outside of form by repelling elements is seen in the young man affected while on an excursion from his form, related in the chapter on Duality.

Disembodied spirits that are inthralled by earthly

conditions carry with them often a low state of moral feeling. Those who are unhappy are apt to show delirium. Those who are not fixed in one sphere or the other can not realize or take in the spirit-life. The changes they have made are between two conditions. More especially those that have been instantly sent out — for instance, by a great calamity — will be for a time wild and frantic, their ideas being disconnected and untruthful. This is so manifest it requires no proof, but is a demonstrated fact that it belongs to the spirit-self. In the higher spheres, as spirit loses the condition of earth and becomes more spiritual, no delirium is shown: for this reason, it may be said that delirium belongs to earthly conditions.

Insanity is purely and absolutely a condition of mentality. There may be a softening or inflammation of the organic structure of the brain ; but this is disease, not dementa. In fact, there may be a perfectly normal, healthy state of the brain-structure, and insanity exist. If it is considered that the brain-substance can not think, will, nor plan ; that it is not the acting intelligence in man, only an organ for a special purpose, — it is absurd to say the brain is insane, more than to say the heart, the stomach, is insane. If disease exist, there may be delirium or unconsciousness, but not dementa. Insanity comes from the condition in the spirit in reality, and exhibits itself in as many forms as it has causes. It may be an overtaxing of the intellectual capacity, domestic cares, or unhappy feelings, disappointment in business or love, remorse, jealousy, or revenge ; or it may be a weakening of the intellectual power itself not able to keep up with the requirements of mentality. Again : the spirit may be turned to acting in a perverted groove or channel, and this perversion becomes its normal state. This is the most permanent form of derangement.

There is a form of demoniac obsession, as well as the influence and elements of disembodied mind, that will act and show violent insanity; but I have never found such permanent, but am convinced that such foreign element would not continuously to any length of time keep control.

Insane persons are conscious of their condition, yet not able to restrain or overcome the difficulty. They realize, remember, and distinguish persons, as well as do those of sound minds: therefore they should be kindly and considerately treated. And more especially is this true where there is a fixed normal state. As this is a perverted state of mentality, if long continued it is an injury to the intellect and progress of the spirit by loss of opportunity all require in external life. For this reason, the mind will show its weakness for a time beyond the earth-life. But in time this is dispelled; and as the scenes of earth fade, and finally disappear, it regains strength and clearness. That there is a vast number of disordered, disembodied minds in close proximity to earth, is a greater truth than is generally supposed.

REST, SLEEP, AND DREAMING.

Rest is cessation from activity. It may be said, Nature never rests; which is true in regard to her ceaseless movements in each and all directions: but in Nature's works there are rests. The shrubs, plants, trees, do not ceaselessly grow, bloom, nor bear fruit. There is rest, decay, and rebuilding, continually.

Soul and intelligence are not Nature in the same sense. There is an independence here which Nature does not wholly control, although there are subjecting conditions to Nature's laws. This intelligent life-essence is the principle designated soul. Whether this principle is superior to Nature is an open question. The true relation existing between nature and soul will be best understood to say one acts in harmony with the other.

Intelligence, or properly the mind, can not be in ceaseless activity more in one condition than in another. As we find on earth, the mind will not sustain ceaseless action, and must have times of rest ; even the same in another sphere, rest is required, and commands itself. Why it is a necessity of mind to rest, I, perhaps, could not satisfactorily show ; but it is a universal demand of entities. It only varies according to circumstances and conditions of individuals.

The rest may be a torpor, an unconsciousness ; or it may be thoughtless inactivity, — an unconcerned listlessness for the time being. But, with those of earth, regular and fixed time is established, and takes the form of sleep.

Sleep differs from rest in this. It is the suspension of the voluntary exercise of the powers of the body and mind ; it is the closing of external senses : yet the mind may have some susceptibility, as is shown in dreams.

That the conditions of sleep depend on the state of both the mental and physical is well known. That it is common to all animal life is also well known. But the best pathologists living will not give a true statement of what causes sleep : they only see the state, the effects, and say it is forgetfulness, or a closing of the senses.

In the chapter on " Occult Forces in Man " a description is given of the structure of the brain, and the abiding-place of the soul in the centre of the whole. The upper brain, or cerebrum, is the intellectual brain entirely, and rests completely during sleep ; while the cerebellum, or lower brain, is the nerve-centre. Every part of the nervous action reflects to this lower brain, and keeps it in rapport with the whole structure continually. When one goes to sleep with no mental or physical disturbance, the spirit likewise takes up a thoughtless listlessness, closes the external senses, and sound sleep is the result. But let the mind be disturbed from some cause according to circumstances, where then is sleep? What is the mind? It is the spirit in the brain; and that can not take rest from its cares, worriments, or troubles: consequently there is no sleep.

It has been shown before that the spirit is the sensorium, sensitive to the vibration of a nerve through the lower brain. If there is such a disturbance and constant vibration, rest is impossible to the spirit; and wakefulness is the result.

The spirit in sleep is not wholly torpid nor insensible; and when a disturbed, troubled part of the body exists, there will be partial consciousness of the same in sleep. This produces dreams, most likely of a tired, troubled character. In fact, the sensorium is much affected by the conditions of the physical during sleep.

There are many causes for dreams outside of the physical conditions. There may be whisperings from intelligences. Disembodied spirits may be near, and cast some influence, or communicate. But the most common is, that mind acts on mind throughout space. Like a sensitive plate, one may receive the reflection of another mind from any plane of action. This will produce cloudy, irregular dreams, without meaning or sense. Unless dreams are vivid and impressive, they are without purpose. When they are intended for a purpose, there will be a waking-up from sleep, because the spirit will be vividly reminded of it.

That the spirit may leave the form, and take excursions in sleep, has been shown in reality.

VALEDICTORY.

In taking leave of our reader, it must not be thought that the subject-matter is exhausted in all its bearings. Not so. But enough has been written to impart some slight insight into truths that may be considered to be of the greatest importance to man, and yet which are but little understood.

All I have presented are facts, not conjectures. It is absolute knowledge, not hypothesis, the seeker after truth wants. I can only say, that, at any time when there was a doubt or uncertainty on a point, I would wait and ask for information, and receive an audible reply coming from distant spheres.

I trust that what I have written may not be in vain; that some may be profited by the same ; and that the lessons herein conveyed will be seed sown to future knowledge that will permeate the human family, and bear fruit to the good of all.

If this small work finds favor, I will give another relating to the next sphere after death, showing that there are occult forces moving the soul of man beyond the grave, — the next most important condition to know, of which all the ideas given convey but the smallest fractional part of the truth. When man learns how the conditions of this life affect another state of being, he will be amazed to look at himself.

A short supplement on our solar system, given directly by the higher intelligences, is presented as the concluding chapter of this work.

OUR SOLAR SYSTEM.

Our solar system, in all its grandeur, all its immensity, all its sublimity, is not understood by the minds of earth.

There is a law in its movements and relation to the whole
creation not comprehended by the denizens of earth.
We can here convey but few *minutiœ* of the truth relating
to it; but will commence with the earth, as that is the
most important for man to know, and go outward.

The centre of the earth is largely composed of electricity and mercury. With these elements — for they are
elements in nature — there are movement and friction; and
a momentum is given to the whole body, producing diurnal
motion. There are other laws that operate on bodies in
motion; but the main force is from the centre to the cir-
cumference.

It is not positive, but it is supposed that all planets are
moved and acted upon by the same laws and elemental
principles. Therefore the earth is electrical; and this
condition comes to the surface, the external. From this
it will be seen, as we proceed, that heat, or the effects of
heat, is produced from the earth itself. As you go from
the surface of the earth into the atmosphere, you will find
that all its elements, gases, matter, have passed into the
atmosphere by evaporation and combustion. Its woods,
coals, oils, metals, have escaped by this process into the
atmosphere, and so into space, as ethereal gaseous matter,
to fill and take their places again in some other nubilous
formation in space. So every thing from earth may be to
some extent represented in other formations. This is the
law of all the planets alike.

The atmosphere partakes of all these conditions, and has
the electric elements of the earth in it.

The annual motion is given by another power from the
sun. This centre is the magnetic attraction of this system: the same it governs to an extent that cannot be
clearly explained. From this solar centre comes the magnetic current that acts on all these bodies.

That the earth is being consumed is true. Every lamp, fire, and furnace is contributing to this result. All its woods, coals, oils, minerals, extracted and given to furnaces and fires, are consuming it, lessening its bulk and matter, which can never be restored in the same body. It is slow combustion, and the inhabitants of earth are accelerating the process of its change.

The sun is not a body of heat, nor is it of the same appearance the eye sees it through the atmosphere. It does not shine : it looks to spirit, or in space, like a body of crimson light, as you would see it through a smoked glass, or as it is seen to set at sea. Its shiny, glaring, dazzling look comes from its effect on the electric atmosphere. Its magnetic currents, flowing through this vaporous channel, draw out the electric forces of earth, which give to it its appearance as well as its heat. It is in accordance with the position of the earth, its incline, and the angles and direction of these currents, that the seasons are made.

The sun is a centre of spirit-strength and magnetic force to every thing it reaches. Its size is very extended, even to spirit-sight. It is growing, and not diminishing. Its inner elements it is not essential for us to describe. It is spiritual, magnetic ; and all the planets move by its force. At the same time, all the planets are in a ratio advancing toward it.

It has been recently demonstrated, by calculation after the transit of Venus, that the earth was some millions of miles nearer the sun than before calculated, and was approaching it. (The writer has not the figures at hand, but saw it so stated.) The interior planets have been once as far removed as any of the most distant. As planets approach the centre, they become less in size, and more spiritual. Therefore the interior planets are more advanced in spiritual conditions than the earth.   Venus is said to be in beautiful spiritual condition.

It is sometimes said these inside planets are younger ; that planets are projectiles from the sun, offsprings of it ; and that Mercury is the infant child.   Not so.   All facts, and the tendency of the laws of these bodies and their motions, are proofs to the contrary.   There is inconsistency in such a supposition as well.

It is the rule laid down in astrology, that Mercury is the intellectual planet ; that Mercury, ascending or ruling at the nativity of a person, will give intellectual bias to that person's elements.   This is not denied.   Is it consistent to suppose that the infant, the least advanced, the one under surveillance, could be the intellectual superior, — would rule the intellectual spirit of one born under its auspices?   It is evident, either the rule or the statement of its position is misstated.   Mercury is the most advanced, the nearest to its transition, in accordance with the law of advance to the sun.   There is a great mistake made to associate great bulk, matter, and volume of planets with fineness, superior spirit, and intelligence : on the contrary, as they lose in grossness, they become more spiritualized.   That these interior planets are not explored is because they surpass us, and spirit cannot go beyond its sphere.   No inhabitant of earth could reach them.   Whatever space outside may be seen belongs to lower grades.

There is another planet next the sun, never yet found through astronomical observation ; but it is so near to the centre, that it may be incorporated with the sun.

Satellites are the offspring, the children, of the planet they follow.   They are the result of its evaporation and elements escaping in its condensation : they partake of its conditions, and are magnetically connected with it.   In time, as there is less evaporation, the satellites become less, and scatter into space : this is done by their dissolving and gaseous escapement.

The interior planets have no satellites at this time, while the farther removed have more as they throw off a larger amount of matter. The earth has had eight of these offspring in the far-distant past. They only show greater productiveness in a planet, and in its advancing age they are lost.[1]

The satellites are not solid earthy bodies, but more of a gaseous element, — water, ice, lime, — and have no atmosphere, therefore are not inhabited by intelligent beings ; but a certain species or kind of moving things are there.

Now we will take the reader outward, called superior, but in reality younger, cruder, and more expansive, as well as distant space, and begin with formation.

All the consumption of matter by combustion, decomposition, and evaporation, causes a gaseous escapement, which passes into space, and becomes ethereal matter. This will accumulate in nubilous bodies, and, when it becomes dense, will congeal. Thus a nubilous body is put in motion. Motion gives rotundity, and the attraction of its own system keeps it in its orbit. In this way every particle of escapement of gross matter from the planets is taken up, and re-formed in some other body.

It has the elements and electrical principles common to all. The new body is usually of great bulk, watery or gaseous, and is slow to become solidified. For ages incal-

---

[1] Since this was put in manuscript, a brilliant astronomical discovery was made in regard to the planet Mars ; namely, that this planet is accompanied by two satellites. On the 16th of August, 1877, at the Naval Observatory, D.C., Professor Hall first observed one. After several days' observation, assisted by other professors, a second satellite, much closer to the planet, was found. Thus, before this work could go to press, the assertion that all the outside planets are accompanied by more than one satellite is verified by this noteworthy discovery of science. Prior to this, Mars was not known to be accompanied by any satellite.

culable a change has been going on in its composition. As
this is done, it contracts, grows less and less in bulk, and
finally takes its place with solid bodies. All the seed-
germs of that from which it escaped are contained in this
nubilosity, and a repetition is made of what has previously existed. These bodies form on the outside because
there is space, and the ethereal vapor goes to the circum-
ference of its system in escaping. After they condense,
and begin to contract, they lose; and the satellites are
thrown off as a surplus of gaseous matter. As they
advance to the centre, and are contracting, they are, in the
course of time, so lessened as to lose all the ethereal mistiness, and then become solid bodies. It is their law to
advance and contract, this is inevitable, while slowly and
by stages the forms of life are taken upon them; always
the lowest first, and the higher as progress is made. This
progress is so exceedingly slow, that time can hardly be
thought of. There is a body not so very ethereal forming
at this time that fills an immensity of space, which in time
will be recorded as a newly-discovered body. Then, in
due time, it will fill our place; and thus throughout the
whole universe change is continually in progress.[1]

The more distant and removed a body is from the
centre, the less progressed and spiritually conditioned it is.
It is then the law, in these circles round the sun, to move
inward, — to advance to the sun-centre. As this is done,
there is more of the magnetic currents and influence of
the solar conditions which are intelligent. From this it
can be relatively estimated what the intellectual or intelligent development of the exterior planets of this system
are. We shall not undertake to analyze the individual
bodies; space would not allow; and it would be un-

---

[1] Since writing this passage, a new planet is reported to have been discovered
in July or August, 1877; its location and movements noted.

necessary. Some of them are well inhabited; others are not.

A thousand years are but the fraction of a second in time in the movements and results of these bodies. Thus it is impossible to note any thing like time in regard to them. The age of your own sphere can be judged by this general rule. How many must have come and gone from it during the eight millions of years it has been inhabited by animal life! Its destiny is great. The law of progress rules it: therefore it must advance, and not recede. It will grow less as it is consumed, and more spiritual as it nears the sun. In time it will be small as the least, and nearest the centre.